The Music of Failure

The Music of Failure

BILL HOLM

Foreword by Jim Heynen

Afterword by David Pichaske

University of Minnesota Press

MINNEAPOLIS · LONDON

THE FESLER–LAMPERT MINNESOTA HERITAGE BOOK SERIES
This series reprints significant books that enhance our understanding and appreciation of Minnesota and the Upper Midwest. It is supported by the generous assistance of the John K. and Elsie Lampert Fesler Fund and the interest and contribution of Elizabeth P. Fesler and the late David R. Fesler.

Thanks to Kim Hodgson, Nancy and Joe Paddock, and Minnesota Public Radio for material broadcast in a tape on Minneota.

Some of these pieces previously appeared in *Minnesota Monthly, Crazy Horse, Spoon River Quarterly, Milkweed Chronicle, Poets of Southwest Minnesota, Poetry Outloud, The Gathering Post,* and from Westerheim Press.

Photographs by Tom Guttormsson

Originally published in 1985 by Plains Press, Marshall, Minnesota
First University of Minnesota Press edition, 2010

PUBLISHED BY THE UNIVERSITY OF MINNESOTA PRESS
111 Third Avenue South, Suite 290
Minneapolis, MN 55401-2520
http://www.upress.umn.edu

Library of Congress Cataloging-in-Publication Data

Holm, Bill, 1943–2009.
  The music of failure / Bill Holm ; foreword by Jim Heynen ; afterword by David Pichaske.
  — 1st University of Minnesota Press ed.
    p. cm. — (The Fesler–Lampert Minnesota Heritage Book series)
  ISBN 978-0-8166-7008-6 (pbk. : alk. paper)
  1. Holm, Bill, 1943–2009. 2. Poets, American — 20th century — Biography.
  3. Minnesota—Social life and customs. I. Title.
  PS3558.O3558Z46 2010
  811'.54 — dc22
  [B]   2010002142

Printed in Canada on acid-free paper

The University of Minnesota is an equal-opportunity educator and employer.

17 16 15 14 13 12 11 10   10 9 8 7 6 5 4 3 2 1

THE AUTHOR AND PHOTOGRAPHER DEDICATE
THIS BOOK TO THE MEMORY OF JONA AND BILL HOLM
AND ADA AND RAGNAR GUTTORMSSON.

CONTENTS

FOREWORD

Jim Heynen

With special thanks to John Rezmerski, David Pichaske,
Lawrence Owen, and Marcy Brekken

HATCHING A BIG ONE

Shortly after Bill Holm's death in February 2009, like so many of his friends and admirers, I turned to his writing for solace. When I pulled down a copy of the 1985 Plains Press edition of *The Music of Failure*, I found this inscription:

> Xmas/ 85
>
>   for Jim Heynen
> The music in Sioux Center is in the same key as in Minneota!
> Thanks for your house which hatched the essay.
>   Affectionately, Bill Holm

The house he referred to was in Port Townsend, Washington, where I lived at the time—a long way from my boyhood stomping grounds near Sioux Center, Iowa, and equally far from his Minneota, Minnesota. A few years before the publication of *The Music of Failure* Bill had come to visit, and when my family and I needed to be away for the weekend, he asked whether he could stay to read and write.

When we returned, he looked exhausted and exalted. There on our living room table, two blocks from the Strait of Juan de Fuca, he had hooked a big one. But instead of a fishing metaphor, when he looked back on the experience of writing that first draft of the title essay, he used a farm metaphor—he had not *caught*, he had *hatched* a big one. He held out a stack of long yellow legal pad paper on which a ballpoint pen had spent two days dancing with a furious urgency to compose the first draft of the essay. Bill was holding the fledgling version of what many now see as one of the most significant American essays of the late twentieth century.

This little book is both early and vintage Holm. The title essay is its centerpiece, but the other essays (including some very brief tributes and reflections) tell us much about the kinds of subjects he will revisit often. Together, these early essays are a key to Bill's work, both his prose and poetry—and to the man as well. The seeds, the vision, and many of the subjects and themes that would be the focus of his illustrious career are all here: his respect for place with its history and ghosts, his abhorrence of greed and pretense, his distrust of power and the powerful, his respect for the humble and powerless, and, always, the importance of music, which, he writes in "The Music of Failure," "remained the true channel to the deepest part of my feeling life."

The value, the *music*, of failure lies in an individual's and a nation's willingness to "see the death" in things, to face the truth of our personal and national history, and to embrace the beauty that accompanies honest and clear vision. Bill was anything but a cynic, but you don't find much pop psychology in his work. No feel-good shortcuts. Finding the music of failure is a life's work, which he clearly believed meant opening oneself—mind, heart, and senses—to all that the messy world has to offer. One cannot be open to the world under the yoke of arbitrary power: it is bad largely because it restricts a person's own experience.

When *The Music of Failure* first came out, it startled many of us. How could anything so modest and local have such a grand sweep? It was like hearing a Brandenburg Concerto coming from a penny whistle. The small-press modesty of the publication was typically Holmsian: from the outset of his writing career, he wanted to speak to a larger audience from his very particular place on earth, to find the whole world in the grain of sand that was his local habitation. If someone else hadn't done it, he would have created the slogan "Act locally, think globally."

MINNESOTA ICON

At the time of his death, Bill Holm's reputation had moved well beyond the local. He had become one of the most visible and admired writers in Minnesota. Hundreds called him "friend." I can't imagine how many came to know him in his world travels, which ranged from his ancestral home of Iceland to Madagascar and China—and numerous points in between. Thousands knew him from the classroom. Thousands heard him on radio broadcasts or saw him on public TV. Thousands more saw him perform onstage, in auditoriums, at commencements, and at an assortment of special events that called for "something different." Bill Holm was "something different." He was our lyrical polemicist, railing against the false optimism and the depleted values of American culture, sometimes sounding like the Old Testament Amos and other times adding verses to the Song of Solomon. When he was in high dudgeon, he could say what many of us didn't dare to say—and with the clarity and wit of a Mark Twain. At other times, in Whitmanesque flourishes he extolled beauty and virtue wherever he saw them.

We treasured Bill because we knew his love of the beautiful was deeper than his hatred of the ugly. For all his frequent bluster, he was an unassuming man who mingled as comfortably with day laborers as he did with politicians, musicians, academics, scientists, and his fellow writers.

What some of us already know, and what many more will discover over the coming years, is that this very public person was, in the private company of his ballpoint pens and yellow legal pads, a consummate artist whose work deserves to be read as much as the work of the people whom he most admired. Informed readers will not be surprised that his influences and models go back to junior high, where he first discovered Thomas Paine. They will not be surprised that he idolized D. H. Lawrence for his exuberance and satiric bite. Thoreau is an inspiration, but, as his writer friend John Rezmerski points out, "more for the quality of his prose than for his ideas." Ed Abbey? Certainly, Bill could offer parallel jeremiads, but his basic congeniality somehow made his judgments sound less harsh. Many names could be mentioned—Emerson, Swift, Chaucer—but always Whitman, and for many reasons. Bill shared both Whitman's admiration for the founding vision of America and his dismay over America's failure to live up to that vision. He emulated Whitman's grandeur and elegant clarity. He shared Whitman's respect for the dead and what we can learn from them by carrying them inside ourselves. Still, Bill's work was not markedly imitative of those whom he admired. He didn't copy, he synthesized. There was no one like him. Harrison Salisbury wrote, "Bill Holm is a Minnesota marvel." He was, and he was ours.

THE BARD OF MINNEOTA

Walden was to Thoreau what Rainy Lake was to Ernest Oberholtzer and what Iceland was to Bill Holm: places of inspiration or refuge that were not home. Bill's Minneota is quite another story. A nondescript little town in southwestern Minnesota whose water tower you can spot from ten miles away, a town with extremely affordable housing and a population of about 1,500 (a quarter of whom are over age sixty-five), it is the place of Bill's ancestral Icelandic immigrant roots. It's the kind of peaceful little town that makes old people feel restful and young people feel restless. He wrote in "The Music of Failure," "At fifteen, I could define failure fast: to die in Minneota, Minnesota." Bill did leave, but he also returned.

Minneota sometimes was his albatross but more often his angel. His relationship with his beloved birthplace reminds me of an odd relationship between a man and a rat from my Iowa farm days. An old farmer would go out to a shed behind his house after supper to wash eggs and tell stories. I'd go to watch and listen. With regularity, a rat came up through a hole in the floor. The old man would utter a mild curse and throw an egg at the rat. He always missed. When the egg splattered against the wall, the rat graciously ate the egg. Over time, the well-fed rat looked quite healthy with its shiny slick coat. Minneota was to Bill what that rat was to the old man. I listened to him fling many a verbal egg at Minneota. Minneota ate those delicious eggs and came back for more—even going so far as to initiate "Boxelder Bug Days," a festival in honor of Bill's book *Boxelder Bug Variations*. Minneota, especially its weather, was a place that Bill loved to hate and hated to love. In truth, they had a lovely and long-lasting simpatico affair. Minneota has the very qualities Bill aspired toward in his life and writing. It is an honest place. It has clarity. It honors and learns from its dead. It doesn't have a haughty side, and it is quite capable of eating any egg you throw at it.

MORE LIGHT!

Conscience

is sun awareness

—D. H. Lawrence

"How They Die"

They dry up,

turn into light.

—from *Boxelder Bug Variations*

Bill Holm liked to see where he was going. He preferred vistas to enclosures. Forests, and the shaded darkness that accompanies them, made him uncomfortable. Though he was a self-confessed claustro-phobic, the significance of this preference is much richer than simple avoidance of confinement: it reveals a deep desire for the clear, long view. Much of his work adheres to this notion. In "Horizontal Gran-deur," an essay in this collection and one of the first long essays Bill wrote, he distinguishes between the prairie eye and the woods eye: "The prairie eye looks for distance, clarity, and light . . ." Light, of course, means more than sunshine to Bill, and it means anything but an optimistic smiley face. Nor does he seek the artificial light "Up in the cities" where "the freeway lights burn all night" (*The Dead Get By with Everything*, 30). His prairie vision seeks to see things without distortion. The application of the metaphor moves into his personal aesthetics: "The prairie eye looks for usefulness and plainness in art and architecture . . . " Although he says that one kind of seeing is no better than the other, just different, his preference in this essay and in much of his work is apparent: he associates prairie eyes with patience and effort, the qualities that he finds lacking in most of American culture with its hunger for one quick thrill after another. And the same enlightened eye that will turn its Viking warrior focus against corruption is the enlightened eye that celebrates what is good: "Trust a prairie eye to find beauty and understate it truthfully." He called his partner and wife, Marcy Brekken, his fleur du Nord. Lovely without pretension, she was his flower of the north, a model of what he sought in people and the world; like Holm, she is a person of the prairie.

In his final collection of essays, *The Windows of Brimnes: An American in Iceland* ("a place of seemingly endless light"), Bill laments leaving the landscape that provided "an opera of light and bird cries," but in this book he also celebrates the guiding lights in the past: in the branches of his own family tree and in Icelandic history and sagas. In tracing his own family roots, he asserts, "Part of the passion for genealogy, the uncovering of ancestors, comes, at its most intelligent end, from a desire to slice through the fog" (104).

In *The Music of Failure* the guiding lights, and often the pursuit of clarity in expression as well as vision, show themselves in tributes to people he admires, including his longtime friend John Allen, his gardening cousin Daren Gislason, and—notably—the strong-handed Bill Holm Sr.

Are there contradictions in Bill's aesthetic? No doubt. The late editor and poet Bill Truesdale asked how someone could preach the gospel of plainness and simplicity while having such a baroque imagination. If accused of contradicting himself, Bill Holm most likely would have echoed Whitman: Do I contradict myself? Very well, then, I contradict myself.

TELLING THE DANCER FROM THE DANCE

Bill Holm and his writing were one. Few writers manage to have their life and writing perform the same symphony, and it's an admirable kind of harmony. I think of the poet William Stafford with his polished reserve and aggressive neutrality: to know his writing was to know the man. Stafford's daily speech resembled his poetry, and his poetry flowed easily from his ordinary life. The same harmony between life and art was true for Bill: the person who spoke exuberantly about poetry, the natural world, music, or politics was the same person you meet in his writing.

Bill Holm was a large man with a huge personality. Friend and poet Barton Sutter called him "the polar bear of American literature." Robert Bly compared him to the large-bodied eighteenth-century Dr. Johnson, holding forth in passionate literary conversation. He was, in all venues, a formidable presence. Before his hair turned gray, he resembled a redheaded Santa Claus who could fill in as a Viking warrior in the off-season—and the role switch would not require a new costume, only a mood change. Bill's twinkling and beneficent Santa Claus face could transform quickly into a fierce Viking warrior if the enemy used money as a weapon to glorify himself or oppress others, or if the weight of inanity in any situation simply became too overwhelming. A rumor circulated that the Minnesota Vikings asked Bill to be their mascot, a rumor he never affirmed or denied but one that he must have enjoyed.

A bit of a Luddite, he never used a typewriter or computer ("I'm not a plug-in tech-man at all," he commented in his "Artist's Statement" for the tribute published by the McKnight Foundation when he was named its 2008 Distinguished Artist), and he despised TV unless it conveyed a noteworthy movie. He lived in a tilting old Minneota house and drove bulky used cars, but spent more money on books and music collections than most people spend on food. He had a harpsichord, a clavichord, and two pianos—one a $20,000 Yamaha grand piano that he inherited from his friend Mike Doman (see *Playing the Black Piano*) and for which he had to buy a separate small house with floorboards that could hold its weight. He had enough published music stacked on bookshelves to keep two pianists playing nonstop for a decade. The combination of extravagance and frugality characterized the man and his life. Harmony within paradox? More like Bach's contrapuntal twists.

The fuse of Bill's tolerance and patience grew short in a hurry if he smelled the rat of presumptuousness or the skunk of stupidity. He was known to whirl on his heel when entering a restaurant where the jukebox music diminished that most glorious form of human expression into silliness, especially if set to a volume that made conversation impossible. One of his dear friends once said that he could "make things that are not all right seem all right," but more often he could make things that were not all right face the truth of his fulminations on the spot. Politically, he was hard to pin down. He despised the hard-nosed right-wing politics that confined wealth to the wealthy and fostered a countrywide atmosphere of meanness and bellicosity. But he could castigate comfy liberalism and political correctness, too. He mocked liberal fads, whether in flavored lattes or the latest exercise machines. He applied Whitman's "Obey little" not only to corrupt right-wing power but also to the fashionable liberal mandates of the day: "Virtuous eating infects Americans at the moment" (*The Heart Can Be Filled Anywhere on Earth*, 207).

Bill was strong-willed and opinionated, but charming. Sometimes his ideas could sound so outlandish that one might question his intelligence. Big mistake. His intellect was as formidable as his physique. His memory was encyclopedic, packed with memorized poems and music and data on an assortment of topics. Though he disdained all competitive parlor games except bridge (and occasionally poker), he would have made a challenging competitor in a quiz game show—so long as the topic was not pop culture.

With a personality as pronounced as Bill Holm's, it can be hard to separate the dancer from the dance. You can always cheat by going back to any of the many taped videos or oral recordings so that you can reimagine the dancer, but those of you who did not have the honor of knowing him in the flesh will come to know the man when you read what he has written. In reading him, you will find the work of someone who explores life's greatest mysteries in clear and lively language, rich with wit and metaphor, electrified by passion. You will see that he has the intellect to make informed allusions to the large worlds of history, geography, nature, music, and literature. In reading this book and the rest of his work, you will come to know the same person so many knew and miss more with every passing day.

LIVING HIS CREED

> For it is life we want. We want the world, the whole beautiful world, alive—and we alive in it. That is the actual god we long for and seek, yet we have already found it, if we open our senses, our whole bodies, thus our souls.
>
> —"Artist's Statement" in *Bill Holm: 2008 Distinguished Artist*,
>   The McKnight Foundation

> Listen as long as you can;
> sing whenever the right tune
> arrives inside you.
>
> —"Magnificat," in *Playing the Black Piano*

The last sentence in the title essay of *The Music of Failure* reads, "The heart can be filled up anywhere on earth." In 1996, that sentence made its way into the title of another collection of essays, *The Heart Can Be Filled Anywhere on Earth*. Deleting "up" from the title was probably the result of a keen editorial eye and a good ear for sentence rhythm, but I like the original, more Holmsian line: you don't just fill a heart, you fill it *up*!

Bill Holm lived life with gusto. Someone said he lived with one foot always planted firmly on the accelerator. Some might say he overindulged. He honored those skeptics by making fun of his own girth: "Jolly old St. William with his marsupial paunch full of the gifts of a lifetime of cream and butter, and the fat on roasts, and whiskey and chocolate—the sweet gifts a benevolent god gives us to take and eat, rewards for braving a life in this vale of skinny tears" (*The Heart Can Be Filled Anywhere on Earth*, 203). In private conversations, he might defend some of his habits by saying that they kept him sane and kept him from thinking like a puritan. He once said, "I'm not someone who was cut out to be an abstainer from anything!"

Bill lived his creed. He died at sixty-five having lived more life in those years than most people who make it to 110. His zeal for life was more than indulgent living: it was a religious commitment to celebrate the divine that resides in all things.

Here are a few snapshots.

Bill cooking and serving fresh pheasant in slivovitz and cream sauce.

Bill sampling a single malt scotch and asking for a "bump" more.

Bill in a bookstore holding up and shouting the merits of someone's book to all who will listen.

Bill striding to the front of a small-town community hall to play

Joplin on an out-of-tune piano—and switching to another key signature to avoid hitting too many sour notes.

Bill with a microphone in front of a thousand people praising someone else's poetry.

Bill reading—and explaining!—Whitman to wide-eyed and bewildered teenagers.

Bill at his grand piano at 1 a.m., in shorts, with one leg crossed over his knee, an ashtray next to him, playing Haydn.

Bill at the Rusty Corner Cafe ordering a piece of banana cream pie after finishing breakfast.

Bill honoring his wife Marcy's dead cat Buddha by preserving it in the freezer until the Minneota soil thawed enough to allow a proper burial.

Bill sneering at a window display of exercise machines.

Bill visiting his cousin Daren's lavish garden.

Bill in a circle of friends, listing the crimes of the Bush administration.

Bill Holm at full bore lived as religiously consistent with his own beliefs as the devoutly private monk in his cloister. We didn't see the private Holm in his many cloisters, many of them in places quite different from Minneota, where he worshipped with ballpoint pen and yellow legal pad, composing his music of failure into elegant prose.

: The Music of Failure

THE GRAND TOUR

I

Farmers go to bed early, or at least used to when I was a boy. Small towns in Minnesota close by six, the cafes frequently at four. People eat at home, where it doesn't cost money. By ten, silent streets, only the liquor store open, its lonesome Hamm's sign proclaiming a few still up. Nothing but blue flickering TVs behind drawn blinds, and a random pattern of yard lights stretching off onto the prairies. By midnight, nothing. Drive on county roads, and you imagine trolls have kidnapped the human race, leaving only electricity behind. Your headlights are a ship's beacon, lighting up a few breakers on the grass ocean, as the car rocks along toward whatever port you have business in. I like driving late at night on those roads without traffic. It provides me with a valuable corrective against human arrogance.

I drove home from dinner in Willmar, a town about eighty miles northeast of Minneota, in the middle of a warm September night last year. The small grain was in, the last hay mowed and baled, and corn and soybeans breathed heavily for their final ripening. Soon this land would be plowed, black, frozen, a factory waiting to be turned on for the spring shift. Nothing to eat then, except in concrete supermarkets five miles apart; no ghosts of grown things sticking up to remind anybody of anything. But for now, the night was hot, dark, humming with cicadas and frogs in the sloughs. The prairie seemed contented having put its humans to bed for a while.

But nothing else slept. Highway 23 and the county roads were like a Mediterranean bazaar, everything asleep during the day's heat, or worried about the danger from the master race, was up now strolling, munching, preening, copulating, bargaining, examining, enjoying. The ditches erupted whenever the headlights peered into them—a half dozen deer by a fenceline, tails cocked; a whole family of raccoons dragging unison stripes behind them, then stopping for a pow-wow; a lone red fox; kamikaze jack-rabbits trying to outrun the headlights; snappers lurching from ditch to ditch; snakes curled on the warm concrete; pocket gophers darting; the white whoosh of a horned owl swooping past the windshield to hunt lunch; and enough skunks to keep you alert and dodging at the steering wheel. For all I know, there may have been coyotes and bobcats watching me; a hundred years ago, maybe a bear or a wolf. Unseen sloughs full of muskrat settled in their domed wattles, while the beavers were up gnawing boxelders, thumping to each other as they tended the water supply. Under it all, woodchucks and badgers burrowed among the night crawlers, and above, invisible in the dark, hawks eyed the action suspiciously like policemen tending the bazaar.

Perhaps bazaar is not the right metaphor. Though night among the non-human has the proper bustle and buzz, no money changes paws. That's human work, daylight work. It is more like a secret cathedral service in a right-wing dictatorship, when the conquered come out to be themselves, sing and celebrate a little freedom. After all, the prairie is their church, their mother, their country, and they had it all long before we came with combines, watershed projects, pickups and shotguns. That makes me, in my Chevrolet, a remnant of the day junta out patrolling. This is not such a cheerful or romantic thought. Consider road kill, pavement littered with fresh corpses, the foolish ones picked off and crushed at random for risking contact, the odor of new dead skunk.

The other sobering thought for humans is how much joy goes on without us, how much life we have been unable, despite strong effort, to bring under our heel. The raccoon and deer and fox make do with night, and get on with it, intending to outlast us. In optimistic moments, I think they will. I hope so.

II

Continue for a while thinking of the Minnesota prairies as a natural cathedral with night services. By day money changers occupy the temple, and to them, there is no sacred place. The world is only real estate, and can be filed at the court house. The divine is entirely abstract, a series of slogans said but not believed in. Therefore, since the divine has no body, it needs no place to live, need be fed nothing. In the cathedrals of England, for instance, God is fed the dead. Their bones line the walls, are everywhere underfoot. Because of mistakes in human history, these corpses are only important people: generals, nobility, and an occasional safe artist. Never mind: it is a sound idea to hallow a place by putting bones inside it. Some, like Thomas Becket, even die inside cathedrals staining the stones with blood, and that is better yet.

We humans here have a horror of death in houses, and would not dream of going to a Lutheran church where grandmother is buried under the pew to keep you warm and alert during slow passages in the sermon when the building fund comes up. We hide hospitals and graveyards, sanitize the interiors of churches with cheerful posters announcing that we are God's people and he loves us lots. These posters do not mention some of the surprises God has in store for us. I think we want a world without dead in it, so that it can be more easily bought, sold, and used up. Our casual attitude toward disappearing topsoil is difficult to reconcile with what we profess to believe. If we imagine the corpses of a thousand people we loved making a skin on that ground, we would tend it better.

To have a sense of the sacredness of a place involves becoming aware of life that inhabits and dead who sanctify it. Night drives over the prairies are useful in that regard. How can we sell the north eighty when we never really owned it? Who asked the raccoon? Did the fox co-sign?

III

For years, I have been giving whimsical "scenic grand tours" of Minneota, one of the least scenic or whimsical places on the planet. After my night drive (and twenty years of thinking), it occurred to me that I had been gravely serious in everything I said during those tours, despite playing for mostly affectionate laughter. I was trying to explain the sacredness of this not much of a place, my only place on this enormous continent. Those who loved and produced me had not hallowed the rest of it, neither New Jersey, California, Disneyland, nor Washington, D.C., but, for their own private and practical reasons, just this bleak place; it was the only hunk of North America not empty for me. In a mere lifetime, I could hallow no other, and so accepted the groundwork they had already done. Having given up their own sacred places to move here, they had been courteous enough to die and be buried in this ground for my benefit. I now owned a stake in the topsoil, and therefore had better pay attention to it. The raccoon and I were getting on more equal footing, as I started to understand this idea.

I'll give you four examples beyond the obvious ones of family graveyards and homesteads of how the sacredness of a place is either created or discovered, if indeed there is a difference between those two processes, and therefore worth including in the grand tour.

IV

My cousin, Daren Gislason, gardens. That sentence is as inadequate as "Franz Liszt played the piano," "Goya painted," or "Caesar was a soldier." Yet it is a fact, like the others, and the sacred is always born from fact.

He appropriated a stretch of river bank along the Yellow Medicine Creek that three farmers choose not to farm, and there gardens. He does not own his garden, but then no one does.

From the road, you see only a line of trees: cottonwood, boxelder, and willow, then a swelling too small to be called a hill, the size and shape of a burial mound for a second-rate Viking. A ruined couch sits on top of that mound facing west. You watch sunset there, and use wind to escape mosquitoes. After a season or two, mice eat their fill, rain and heat do their job, and the couch disappears back under western Minnesota where it came from. Another equally shabby couch appears, and lasts for another while. Flowers are not the only things grown in gardens; once the process begins, you have nature's munificence on your hands forever. Everything grows in a proper garden except money.

Drive up the narrow farm road cutting 300 yards between tall corn rows. First, you see a half-rusted stock tank full of red and gold moss roses, then a cactus garden. A hundred cactus in this damp place? They are guests, and this is their hotel. They winter indoors, like us. Below the mound sits the corpse of a '39 black Plymouth in the process of rusting back toward earth, but like humans, French cheese, and good beef, growing steadily more beautiful as age and decay overwhelm it. Blue morning glories cover the cracked windshield; moss roses circle the tire-less rims; another cactus garden grows on the sun roof. The Plymouth is a tool shed, left here, like so much of this rusty junk, as a joke. The gardener took whatever chance and affectionate malice left him, decorated it, made it useful, and then let it be.

Beds of iris, tulip, peony, mum, lily, and fifty flowers I don't know are everywhere lined with old beer cans, garnished with iron stove tops, machinery parts, cow skulls, ruined bowling pins, hunks of dead furniture, and cracked toilet bowls. It is amazing how harmoniously iris and scrap iron live together, like and Bach and Jelly Roll Morton played simultaneously but fitting miraculously. Everything has its own use if you look at it right.

Along the creek more flower beds, neatly weeded and decorated. This is Versailles without a palace, therefore without a class structure. Dark leafy openings lead into the grove. It is a cave still alive and moving. After a few hundred trees, you come to a clearing: old Maytag washtubs full of flowers, a half-ruined green wicker chair sitting by the river bank, a book lying open on the seat, more neat paths, more flowers, more old chairs, more books, miles of these paths, acres of flowers, a graveyard of not quite dead furniture, the Library of Congress, the whole universe weeded, planted, mowed, tended, loved, left mostly wild, but civilized a little with everything thrown away and wasted by others from the Pleistocene till now; and everywhere food for birds, jars of peanut butter growing from trees, lumps of suet nailed to wet bark, air loud with grateful music sounded by chickadees, humming birds, nut hatches, blue jays, mourning doves, meadow larks, bluebirds, blackbirds, woodpeckers, crows, herons, sparrows, hawks, and owls; finally a little shack on legs, and a ramp going up. Inside a bed, a chair, a desk, a bowl of peppermints, a pen, and a guest book, in which those who thought they had no poetry in them till they saw this place, sang on paper till it almost drowned out the birds.

Daren Gislason gardens, has always gardened, and sanctified that place. When people visit me in Minneota, I take them there. Once

Daren said to me he knew how often people would be invited to my house by watching me watching them watch his garden. If there was enough intelligence and love in their body when they saw that place, I would give them my house if they wanted it. If they asked who owned it, I never saw them again. That, to begin with, is what I mean by a sacred place. You do not humor unbelievers in the true church; the divine does its own evangelizing.

V

John Allen left Minneota as fast as possible at eighteen to spend the next twenty-five years on the road, exploring and having adventures in the Montana mountains, the Grand Canyon, on a gulf freighter, in Iceland. He walked from Canada to Mexico along the rock spine of the continent, followed autumn south from Lake Itasca to the Gulf of Mexico walking next to the Mississippi, and then followed the next spring north. He works now in Alaska. He carries all his goods in one tattered backpack, ready for the next adventure in fifteen minutes. He is as close as America can come to producing a rootless man: without parents, wife, children, or much family at all, no telephone number or address. IRS doesn't keep track of him. He cannot be reached, though he may reach you if you know him, perhaps even if you don't.

Yet he has a stronger feeling about the sacredness of place than anyone else I've met. He once owned a beagle, his best hiking sidekick, and when a truck got the dog, John Allen buried him on a Montana hill. He visits the dog's grave once a year, bringing artifacts from his travels to leave as grave mound offerings: a rusty Grain Belt can, an oyster shell, a duct-taped tennis shoe, a photograph, a rubber lizard, a greasy menu. Friends invited to the ceremony bring similar gifts; a bottle of bad wine is cracked and drunk after a ritual cap crushing. The dog is praised, the grave straightened and ordered, a song or two sung. Then everyone leaves till next year, feeling slightly richer and happier for having left these sacrifices. Even if you live in a backpack, you carry some sacred places with you.

But he returns to Minneota once a year to visit human graves, see old friends, and tell travel stories. His parents died within a year of each other, and ordered a double gravestone: two names, four dates. In the bustle of that quick succession of funerals, his father's second date went uncarved. Always born in 1911, Leonard had only a hyphen at the end. After a few years, it became apparent to John that no one noticed the mistake. When a family friend finally did notice, she demanded that the stonecarver be summoned, but John refused. He had gotten attached to the missing date; if it was never carved, his father went on still partly alive. When you talk to a second date, don't expect quick answers.

That flawed, incomplete grave becomes hallowed, not for presence, but for absence. It represents human insistence on the peculiar and irregular in a world which uses normality as a blunt instrument; it honors the visible through what is invisible, thus reversing the usual theological process. Huge old elms circled the graveyard, half now dead and burned for firewood, the other half diseased and overdue for cutting. It won't make any difference when they're gone, since air over that place had permanent holes punched in it by elm tops rising into my memory of the prairie sky.

VI

In a country that imagines itself populated by John Doe and Dick and Jane, what a relief to find a graveyard with stones that read Hallgrimur, Vigfus, Adalborg, Metusalem, Gottskalksson, Gislason, Isfeld! They say: we're not melted yet, or if so the job is just finished, and the alloy still smoking. Those are graveyard names next to the Lincoln County

Icelandic church, a bare white wood-frame building visible for miles, the Icelanders having braved wind and built at the top of a ridge of glacial hills.

I took three people there at the end of a warm late fall day ten years ago, showed them the graves, told them a story or two, and then walked them into the church to hear the old reed organ, see sunset through the plain gold windows, and feel the wind that always came indoors with you in that room. By then the church had been closed up for fifteen years, and was covered with thick dust inside. The two Minneapolis friends were actors, a husband and wife, and the third, a woman I didn't yet know well, but had already decided I loved. The couple and I came in first, went immediately to the dusty organ, pulled out the bench, pumped vigorously, and began playing and singing bad gospel tunes and gloomy old Scandinavian hymns. We all felt jocular, pleased with this lonesome place.

In the middle of the fun, we looked up and saw the other woman standing in the pulpit looking pensive, paying us no attention. Come join us and sing up a little "Scandihoovian" salvation, we invited. She ignored us, continued staring out at the empty pews. She dampened our high spirits, and we all fell into uncomfortable silence. One serious human can ruin the whimsy of a whole army.

"There is someone else here," she said in a flat voice. "I was in the room behind the pulpit, the little one with the wash stand and the oak chair and hooks on the wall, just looking around, running my finger through the dust. I sat down in the chair and looked at the window covered with cobwebs and dead flies. Sitting there, I felt the presence of other people around me, a heavyset woman, and an old man, small and bald, dressed for Sunday in a black suit long out of style. He was looking at papers, fingering them, as if thinking. When you began playing that music, they went away."

I shivered, shooing everyone out of the church quickly. The woman described, with extraordinary exactness, Rannveig and Guttormur Guttormsson, the minister of that church for fifty years, and his wife, dead now for almost twenty years, exactly as I saw them every Sunday morning of my boyhood. The woman had never heard them described or even mentioned. She had never been here, and knew me slightly. Though I don't know what love has to do with this experience, I include it in case it is of any use to anyone who might understand what happened in that small room. I know only one thing about it: there is no explanation for what happened, nor any need of one. It was a gift from that place to all of us, and sanctified it beyond its churchness. Should the church burn, or be torn down, and the graveyard plowed up, it would not affect the meaning of that place. Something divine entered partial consciousness that night, and waits patiently to be known more fully. You only move around an event like this, and try to see an outline; it is like trying to build a wall out of fog that will keep cattle in a pasture. Keep trying; it might be possible.

VII

Two blocks from downtown Minneota, in the yard outside a tiny house, stood a tree stump maybe ten feet tall. Swirls like decorations on an old Viking drinking bowl were carved into it. And out of those swirls grew four faces: Thorstein Veblen, Simone de Beauvoir, Jean Paul Sartre and Martin Buber. Visitors to Minneota, driving by it with blank astonishment, asked me, "What the devil was that doing in Minneota of all places?"

"Why not?" I'd reply. "We can read in Minneota, and they sell wood chisels right in the hardware store; a lot of dead trees around, and they're really not much good for firewood." I was not being entirely disingenuous.

That totem to private intellectual life in an unlikely place was the work of Rollie Johnson, a native Minneota Norwegian whose previous labor, aside from reading Veblen, included driving the local milk route until supermarkets put a stop to such service. Rollie began carving at about thirty after cutting down a tree that cast too much shade on his garden. The saw got stuck, and he had to take a chisel to loosen and remove it. The chiseling interested him in some mysterious way that he was never able to explain, even to himself, so he kept at it despite never having had an art teacher tell him how difficult things were.

Since he liked the results, he went on carving till he almost drove his wife out of their tiny house by filling it with busts of Gandhi, Tolstoy, Beethoven, Helen Keller, Mark Twain, Frederick Douglass, and Eleanor Roosevelt; imagined scenarios from *Faust* and *The Wild Duck*; animals inside cages; bears on picnic; ominous turtles; skaters who moved when you touched them; Buckminster Fuller inside a triangle; all the American presidents in one nine-foot row (he stopped it before carving Reagan); heads and bodies of relatives, friends, parents, grade school classmates, town eccentrics, and imaginary characters who represented powerful emotions. He carved elms dead from disease, birch cut for firewood, a butternut communion rail from the old Norwegian church, good oak, soft boxelder, and a piece of lignum vitae, the world's hardest wood, that he whittled to see if indeed it could be done. He carved chess sets with Viking heads, characters off a radio show, communists versus capitalists, farmers versus town merchants, and two opposing football teams. He winched an enormous cottonwood stump off a branch in his yard, and stood on a ladder for the better part of year carving a tender statue of a man and a woman embracing until the wood cracked and he wryly admitted defeat at the hands of nature. His carvings, whatever technical deficiencies they may have had as a result of his being a complete autodidact (in this as in other regards), burgeoned with energy, intelligence, and humor. They were carvings of the interior of his mind, the books he read, the people he knew, his reflections on how the universe is organized. Together they created a garden of wood, a library of wood, a church of wood—any and all these metaphors are true.

He had difficulty selling carvings, either refusing to part with them at all, or charging an outrageously small price. Uncomfortable with selling, he was the world's prickliest marketer. He didn't seem to believe that he owned his own carvings and, therefore, ought not to make money from them. His passion to carve, and discovery of the genius for it caused difficulty in his life so he decided to be done with it. He cut down his first totem, gathered the rest of his work and auctioned it publicly, making the wise capitalist stipulation that he would let it all go, no matter how low the price.

The prices were low enough to satisfy his darkest suspicions, and I think, as I write these words, that he has again tried to give up carving. I own a dozen of those pieces—probably the best, though own is an unsatisfactory word for my relationship to them. They stay in my house for a while, and almost breathe.

I have no idea who now owns the totem, or where it lives, but it must seem strange to have this harbinger planted in your front yard. To be suddenly given the passion for beauty is an uncertain burden, and as easily destroys as enriches whoever receives it. The Northwest Indians knew the power in carving totem images, and were very careful; totem is their sacred word, not ours. Nevertheless, Rollie Johnson's imagining of Thorstein Veblen lives permanently in the imagination of Minneota, even if it now turns to firewood.

VIII

Reading Icelandic sagas, I am struck with the idea that half the experience in the story happens to humans, and the other half to Iceland itself. *Hrafnkel's Saga,* a typical one, is as much about the settling, naming, and hallowing of places in that landscape as it is about Hrafnkel's humiliation and revenge. Here are some sentences that illustrate what I mean:

> *The following winter a foreign bondswoman named Arnthrud died there, and that is why the place has been known as Arnthrudarstead ever since.*

> *The landslide fell on the farmstead killing these two beasts and that is why the place has been called Geitdale ever since.*

> *Hallfred found a drier, but slightly longer way across the moor. This path has been called Hallfredargata ever since, and it can only be used by those who are thoroughly familiar with the moor.*

> *They led the stallion to the bluff, pulled a bag over his head, tied long heavy poles to his flanks, fastened a stone to his neck, and with the poles, they pushed the horse over the cliff. So the horse perished, and the bluff has been known as Freyfaxahamar ever since.*

Most Minneota Icelanders came from the immediate vicinity of that saga. It was their great-grandfather's land, and those place names and stories attached to them are cellular information. A thousand years of legends, corpses, dead goats, stumbling horses, and battles have given human, thus divine life to the most insignificant bog in this part of Iceland. That land belongs not only to the farmer who pastures his sheep on it, but to me because I know the name Freyfaxi's Cliff, and to you if you want it, and to no one.

So where are our sacred places in Minneota, our bone-filled cathedrals, our Freyfaxi's Cliff? I have proposed four: a garden, a gravestone with a missing date, a church where something odd may or may not have happened, and a tree stump first carved, then removed. This is not much of a grand tour, you say; they could probably do better in Nebraska. William Carlos Williams did his best in New Jersey, too. Even the raccoon that got mentioned several pages ago, you add, could probably crank up more than this in pitch dark. These places are only places, you say, and boring ones at that, hardly distinguishable from a million other such places. How is anyone to know about the divinity you work so hard to give them? Aren't they just spots where some colorful character was involved in a memorable anecdote? Why not just leave them be human, plain places, and go to a real Lutheran church where they have stewardship Sunday, or to a Catholic church to hear what people who know better think about abortion and living in sin? If you stayed home at night where you belong, or kept your mind on the road instead of prying in the ditches off highway 23, you wouldn't exaggerate so much.

I have news for those who have a vested interest in maintaining the supernatural bureaucracy that services our well-defended capitalist commune here in America. The divine lives in *all* the human, and the human lives in *all* the world, or nature if you wish, or the planet speeding along under foot if you like that better. Sacredness is unveiled through your own experience, and lives in you to the degree that you accept that experience as your teacher, mother, state, church, even, or perhaps particularly, if it comes into conflict with the abstract received wisdom that power always tries to convince you to live by. One of power's unconscious functions is to rob you of your own experience by saying: we know better, whatever you may have seen or heard, whatever cockeyed story you come up with; we are principle, and if experience contradicts us, why then you must be guilty of something. Power—whether church, school, state, or family—usually does this at first in a charming way while feeding you chocolate cake, bread and wine, advanced degrees, tax shelters, grant programs, and a strong national defense. Only when contradicted does it show its true face, and try to kill you. Instead, kill it inside you fast, and do it whatever damage seems practical in the outer world. Next, put your arms around everything that has ever happened to you, and give it an affectionate squeeze. This is what you will see on your own night drive: your private stash of beloved corpses, your fellow creatures grown into their skins and consciousness in some interesting way; your nonhuman, tax-evading citizens; your patch of garden, where in spite of the county real estate office, you have planted the flag of your own holy empire; every shred of music that goes on sounding in you so that you compose and orchestrate it every day of your life.

The raccoon may then show you a thing or two, even invite you to worship in the grass with him, but the raccoon's church, though we ought to respect it, will not do for us because we are human, and must name our own places from our own experience. I was born at Holnum, an Icelander's farm in Swede Prairie, an immigrant township settled by others first in Yellow Medicine County, named for a Sioux river in North America, mapped by an Italian. My whole history is in those names, and I have no other, nor do I need one. I have bones to prove that it belongs to me.

HORIZONTAL GRANDEUR

For years I carried on a not-so-jovial argument with several friends who are north-woods types. They carted me out into the forests of northern Wisconsin or Minnesota, expected me to exclaim enthusiastically on the splendid landscape. "Looks fine," I'd say, "but there's too damn many trees, and they're all alike. If they'd cut down twenty miles or so on either side of the road, the flowers could grow, you could see the sky, and find out what the real scenery is like." Invariably, this provoked groans of disbelief that anyone could be insensitive enough to prefer dry, harsh, treeless prairies. There, a man is the tallest thing for miles around; a few lonesome cottonwoods stand with leaves shivering by a muddy creek; sky is large and readable as a Bible for the blind. The old farmers say you can see weather coming at you, not like woods, where it sneaks up and takes you by surprise.

I was raised in Minneota, true prairie country. When settlers arrived in the 1870s they found waist-high grass studded with wildflowers; the only trees were wavy lines of cottonwoods and willows along the crooked Yellow Medicine Creek. Farmers emigrated here not for scenery, but for topsoil; 160 flat acres without trees or boulders to break plows and cramp fields was beautiful to them. They left Norway, with its picturesque but small, poor, steep farms; or Iceland, where the beautiful backyard mountains frequently covered hay fields with lava and volcanic ash. Wives, described by Ole Rölvaag in *Giants in the Earth*, were not enamored with the beauty of black topsoil, and frequently went insane from loneliness, finding nowhere to hide on these blizzardy plains. But the beauty of this landscape existed in function, rather than form, not only for immigrant farmers, but for Indians who preceded them.

Blackfeet Indians live on the Rocky Mountains' east edge in northern Montana—next to Glacier National Park. Plains were home for men and buffalo, the source of Blackfeet life; mountains were for feasting and dancing, sacred visions and ceremonies, but home only for spirits and outlaws. It puzzles tourists winding up hairpin turns, looking down three thousand feet into dense forests on the McDonald Valley floor, that Blackfeet never lived there. It did not puzzle the old farmer from Minneota who, after living and farming on prairies most of his life, vacationed in the Rockies with his children after he retired. When they reached the big stone escarpment sticking up at the prairie's edge, one of his sons asked him how he liked the view. "These are stone," the old man said; "I have stones in the north eighty. These are bigger, and harder to plow around. Let's go home."

When my mother saw the Atlantic Ocean in Virginia, she commented that though saltier, noisier, and probably somewhat larger, it was no wetter or more picturesque than Dead Coon Lake or the Yellow Medicine River and surely a good deal more trouble to cross.

There are two eyes in the human head—the eye of mystery, and the eye of harsh truth—the hidden and the open—the woods eye and the prairie eye. The prairie eye looks for distance, clarity, and light; the woods eye for closeness, complexity, and darkness. The prairie eye looks for usefulness and plainness in art and architecture; the woods eye for the baroque and ornamental. Dark old brownstones on Summit Avenue were created by a woods eye; the square white farmhouse and red barn are prairie eye's work. Sherwood Anderson wrote his stories with a prairie eye, plain and awkward, told in the voice of a man almost embarrassed to be telling them, but bullhead-edly persistent to get at the meaning of the events; Faulkner, whose endless complications of motive and language take the reader miles behind the simple facts of an event, sees the world with a woods eye. One eye is not superior to the other, but they are different. To some degree, like male and female, darkness and light, they exist in all human heads, but one or the other seems dominant. The Manicheans were not entirely wrong.

I have a prairie eye. Dense woods or mountain valleys make me nervous. After once visiting Burntside Lake north of Ely for a week, I felt a fierce longing to be out. Driving home in the middle of the night, I stopped the car south of Willmar, when woods finally fell away and plains opened up. It was a clear night, lit by a brilliant moon turning blowing grasses silver. I saw for miles—endless strings of yardlights, stars fallen into the grovetops. Alone, I began singing at the top of my voice. I hope neither neighborhood cows, nor the Kandiyohi County sheriff were disturbed by this unseemly behavior from a grown man. It was simply cataracts removed for the prairie eye with a joyful rush.

Keep two facts in mind if you do not have a prairie eye: magnitude and delicacy. The prairie is endless! After the South Dakota border, it goes west for over a thousand miles, flat, dry, empty, lit by bril-liant sunsets and geometric beauty. Prairies, like mountains, stagger the imagination most not in detail, but size. As a mountain is high, a prairie is wide; horizontal grandeur, not vertical. People neglect prai-ries as scenery because they require time and patience to comprehend. You eye a mountain, even a range, at a glance. The ocean spits and foams at its edge. You see down into the Grand Canyon. But walking the whole prairie might require months. Even in a car at sixty miles an hour it takes three days or more. Like a long symphony by Bruckner or Mahler, prairie unfolds gradually, reveals itself a mile at a time, and only when you finish crossing it do you have any idea of what you've seen. Americans don't like prairies as scenery or for national parks and preserves because they require patience and effort. We want instant gratification in scenic splendor as in most things, and simply will not look at them seriously. Prairies are to Rockies what *Paradise Lost* is to haiku. Milton is cumulative; so are prairies. Bored for days, you are suddenly struck by the magnitude of what has been working on you. It's something like knowing a woman for years before realizing that you are in love with her after all.

If prairie size moves the imagination, delicacy moves the heart. West of Minneota, the prairies quickly rise several hundred feet and form the Coteau. This land looks more like the high plains of Wyoming. Rougher and stonier than land to the east, many sections have never been plowed. Past Hendricks, along the south and west lake shores, things open up—treeless hills with grazing cattle, gullies with a few trees sliding off toward the lake. Ditches and hillsides are a jumble of flowers, grasses, and thistles: purple, pink, white, yellow, blue. In deep woods, the eye misses these incredible delicate colors, washed in light and shadow by an oversized sky. In the monochromatic woods, light comes squiggling through onto a black green shadowy forest floor. My eye longs for a rose, even a sow thistle.

A woods man looks at twenty miles of prairie and sees nothing but grass, but a prairie man looks at a square foot and sees a universe; ten or twenty flowers and grasses, heights, heads, colors, shades, configurations, bearded, rough, smooth, simple, elegant. When a cloud passes over the sun, colors shift, like a child's kaleidoscope.

I stop by a roadside west of Hendricks, walk into the ditch, pick a prairie rose. This wild pink rose is far lovelier than hot-house roses wrapped in crinkly paper that teenagers buy prom dates. The dusty car fills with its smell. I ignore it for a few minutes, go on talking.

When I look again, it's dry, as if pressed in an immigrant Bible for a hundred years. These prairie flowers die quickly when you take them out of their own ground. They too are immigrants who can't transplant, and wither fast in their new world.

I didn't always love prairies. On my father's farm I dreamed of traveling, living by the sea and, most of all, close to mountains. As a boy, I lay head on a stone in the cow pasture east of the house, looking up at cloud rows in the west, imagining I saw all the way to the Rockies and that white tips on the clouds were snow on mountaintops or, better yet, white hair on sleeping blue elephant spines. Living in a flat landscape drove me to indulge in mountainous metaphor, then later discover that reality lived up to it. When I finally saw the Rockies years later, they looked like pasture clouds, phantasmagorias solider than stone.

The most astonished travelers do not come from the Swiss Alps, or the California coast. Only William Carlos Williams, who lived in the industrial prairies of New Jersey, would notice the Mexico of *Desert Music*. A southwest poet with a woods eye would have seen sequaro cactus or medieval parapets. Trust a prairie eye to find beauty and understate it truthfully, no matter how violent the apparent exaggeration. Thoreau, though a woodsman, said it right: "I can never exaggerate enough."

ON TOUR IN WESTERN MINNESOTA, THE POETRY-OUT-LOUD TROUPE READS IN FOUR NURSING HOMES

POETRY-OUT-LOUD——ON TOUR IN MINNESOTA

Some sat in wheelchairs eating their napkins. Others clucked their tongues at Lutherans and Catholics or played fuss-ball in the back bar while the traveling troupe laid on them poetry like a circuit-writer laying on hands.

Folks thought it was nice, but didn't understand why next winter roosters laid eggs, cattle organized a barnyard union, demanded Beethoven on the radio, no more Johnny Cash, snowbanks arranged themselves elegantly into nude women, didn't melt till after April. Maybe anarchists hiding in corners of old stars, they thought, never dreamt it could have been those nice young poets they invited into town.

FOUR NURSING HOMES

Canby

Poets read in the bad wing. A spastic sits up front trying to eat squiggly orange Jell-O without much success. He aims for his mouth, but hits his ear. Jell-O spreads in streaks down already stained pajamas. I read something cheerful. An old man shuffles in from one side with wax paper stuck to his bare foot. The paper squeaks on the tile floor as he walks. He tries to grab the microphone from me. . . .

"What's goin' on here? I got somethin' to say. . . ."

The nurse comes up, embarrassed, and slides him away, wax paper and all. I look down at orange Jell-O, wondering what revelation I missed that would do me any good at ninety.

Dawson

The poets read. There is a faint stink of excrement, ammonia, scented candles, and sugar cookies. She sits quietly for the first stanza, but then screws up her toothless face. . . .

"Shit! It's all shit! They're crazy, crazy! Why do we have to sit here and listen to this shit!"

The dignified Norwegian lady sitting next to her is so used to boredom that she would sit quietly listening to the *Congressional Record* read in Urdu by a computer. She has survived sermons for ninety years, after all. She reaches discreetly for her ear to disconnect her hearing aid.

The crank goes on: "Shit! Nothing but shit!"

She will do no such thing as go gentle into that good night. She gets louder and crankier during my poem. I like her even better. I want to kidnap her, first to Minneapolis, then New York, and wheel her into committee meetings, cocktail parties, congressional hearings, celebrations of the mass, and serious cultural occasions. I may even marry her.

Minneota

In the middle of the reading I decide to smoke and head out the side exit, Yeats and Frost and Minnesota poems still going on behind me. At the door an old man in a wheelchair grabs my hand with an iron grip, strong enough to clutch the reins of horses just about to carry him over the precipice. He looks up at me—"Is the car ready yet?"

The poetry seems not to be working its magic here.

"Yah, they got her all done," I say. "You can pick her up this afternoon."

"Good," he says, seems satisfied.

He settles back in his wheelchair and smiles, thinking about his new fuel pump and the next trip out past the cornfields into the dark.

Olivia

When he reads her own words to her, the old lady's face lights up, palsied hands diseased no longer, now dancer's hands making Egyptian motions. She is Bohemian-Svoboda. Those words move her and why shouldn't they? It's her own life, following pioneer father through deep snow, tiny feet to small to fit in his enormous footprints, feeding chickens, knitting afghans, barn dancing, children leaving, husband dying of his cancer. Now she's alone at ninety, with nothing left but her wheelchair, gone legs, shaking hands, voice deep, manly, strong as if it spoke up from inside her grave already, or as if she had become her husband. The old do this. We all do. When people we love die, we swallow them down inside us, and speak with their voices. Those who love the dead are mediums already, move tables around in darkness everywhere they go.

AN ICELANDIC WOMAN VISITS MINNEOTA

ROUND BARN

She and I go to an old round barn by the river. The barn is full of the
smell of old hay. Wind whistles through missing shingles in the high
dome. Iron stalls are empty now. We see hoofprints on black dirt,
made by cattle long since dead and eaten. From a nail she takes down
a horse harness, leather dried and cracked. "From Iceland," she says,
and caresses it. We walk into the empty hayloft, fifty feet high, shaped
like a cathedral dome. The last sunlight blown into the holes in the
dome by prairie winds shines the floor like a polished ballroom. I walk
under the dome, open my mouth, and sing—an old Italian song about
the lips of Lola the color of cherries. The sound rolls around the dome
and grows. It comes back to me transformed into horse's neighing.

ICELANDIC MUSIC IN TAUNTON, MINNESOTA

She and I go out to a noisy farmer's bar on Saturday night. One old
Icelander, blind drunk now, awestruck at this beautiful woman, comes
up to talk to her. Embarrassed by his own drunkenness, he says everything wrong. "Hey, Billy, who's this one? Half the time you got something black-haired who never says a word." She leans close to his ear:
"Speak some Icelandic to me." He can remember nothing but an old
vulgar song men sing when horses pull them home—half-conscious
in the back of the wagon. The horse plods down the gravel road; the

broken voice rises through the dark from the wagon floor. "I was so drunk, I couldn't tell day from night." It's his father's voice, sixty years ago. When the yellow-haired woman laughs again, he hears his mother putting horses away.

ICELANDIC GRAVEYARD

A woman and I come to an old Icelandic graveyard on a windy tree-less hill in Lincoln County. She has never been here, but sees her own name on every tombstone. Sometimes she died an old lady, sur-rounded by children, like petals around a flower's center. Sometimes she died a child who couldn't talk yet, without God's water on her hairless head. Sometimes her name is spelled right, sometimes not. It is a good thing to die so many times, to feel this often—the death-shudder in the bones—so that now muscles are so practiced at it they do it with a dancer's delicate grace.

THE MOUNTAINS IN LINCOLN COUNTY

Southwest of Minneota, along the county road that goes past the Norwegian Church, land starts rising in tiers, glacial gullies and hills run off on both sides of the road like a giant's stairway, each hill higher, each gully deeper than the last. Look northeast after driving nine or ten miles and you see that you have driven over the top of the Taunton grain elevator, now a few hundred feet below you and 150 feet high. Though the road has not curved, you have driven up a long inclined plane, the spiritual and geological beginning of the Black Hills, the Rocky Mountains, the true west.

On the highest hill, you reach timberline: country opens up, piles of grey stones, thin soil, low scraggly bushes, farms farther apart. These rolling gullies and hills in Lincoln County are the best you can do at feeling alpine tundra here. Had Irish saints moved to the prairies, they would have built beehive huts on these hills, meditating in dry and rarified air, surrounded by grasshoppers and prickly purple thistles, looking down each night at yardlights twinkling on more prosperous farms below and at red lights on elevator tops. As saints everywhere always knew, get up a few hundred feet in order to see good and evil clearly, beyond the distractions of luxuriant growth. Ornamental trees and flowers are not necessary; a few plain stones, thistles, and old boards are best.

WHAT THE PRAIRIE EYE LOOKS FOR IN A MOUNTAIN: CHIEF MOUNTAIN, MONTANA

Chief Mountain stands by itself on the Rockies' edge, a giant knob, square and rough, without roots, graceful slopes, other mountains to protect it, hide it, cover its faults, make it lovely. This plain, Protestant, prairie mountain sticks up unapologetically, even unbeautifully, as if to say to those who come to it:

Here I am, an unassuming rock, pretending nothing, part of nothing, a thing itself. You want softness, trees, wildflowers, alpine lakes, snow glaciers? Go elsewhere. I am what I am.

Climb me and see shivering prairie grass for a thousand miles. Let's have no nonsense about this business of being a mountain. Neither better nor worse than anything else, it is a duty, a responsibility to be shouldered alone, without weeping, complaining, love . . . but with secret joy that moves stones around in moonlight, makes the ghost buffalo dance.

ICELANDERS, BOXELDERS, SOYBEANS, AND POETS

The day before leaving eastern Virginia, I called the telephone company to have my phone disconnected and the bill forwarded to Minneota, Minnesota. I talked to a good-humored black woman and gave her the address. There was a pause. "No street, no number?" None. She asked me to repeat and spell the address. I did. Another pause. "You puttin' me on, man—that a real place?" It is indeed, a place in southwestern Minnesota.

In fact, I was born on a farm eight miles north of Minneota, Minnesota, where my Icelandic grandfather, Sveinn, homesteaded about 1880. The house sat on a hill, surrounded by trees countable on one hand's fingers, and miles of prairie rolling off toward South Dakota. My mother decided I would read books and die without calluses on my hands, but my father would have preferred a son who took slightly more than my minimal interest in cultivating soybeans and repairing combines. At eighteen, what I wanted most to see in the world was the Minneota city limits receding, for the last time, in the rear view mirror of an automobile driving east, to New York, Boston, Washington, where men didn't spit snooze into brass spittoons, wore suits instead of clean bib overalls on Saturday night, where women did not wear shapeless print dresses, or discuss egg prices and the newest hot dish recipe, but were elegant and witty with painted eyebrows and long black gowns.

By gradual steps, I made my way east, through college, graduate school, and into a teaching job next to the Atlantic Ocean, as far east as American consciousness moves. However, a strange thing happened. In addition to the urban culture of martinis and paté, conversation about Italian movies and liberal politics, I found empty-hearted rootlessness, books used as blunt instruments, a sneering disbelief that hayseed farmers had souls, much less intellects. So I began—much to the skeptical amusement of easterners I knew—to tell Minneota stories about fierce winters, eccentric old Icelanders done in by broken hearts, treeless wildflower-covered hills in Lincoln County, pioneer graveyards with peculiar names in Norwegian, Polish, Belgian, or Icelandic; pitching out a ripe hoghouse; soaking tired bones in the claw foot bathtub; country school with brass bell, glass-doored oak bookcase, and half-mooned outhouse; and most of all, the rich variety of characters in small towns, whom one could know, tolerate, and forgive in ways not available to the guarded privacy of the big city. As my mother used to say, Minneota is just like that book by Grace Meticulous *[sic]*—*Peyton Place*—only better; the stories were true, and you knew all the actors.

I meant not to write my autobiography, but to use myself as example, duplicated many times in southwestern Minnesota, of attempted escape from these unlikely prairies, and the discovery, usually after years passing, that for better or worse, you belong in a place, and grow out of its black soil like a cornstalk.

Minneota was a jumble of accents and languages when I grew up there in the forties: burry Icelandic with trilled consonants, Norwegian nasal a's, flat guttural Flemish. You could drive ten miles and hear Polish, German, and Swedish. Northern Europe was here compressed into a thinly peopled county smack in the middle of the American continent. Strangers complained about the prairie's boring monotony,

mile after mile of flat farm fields, but to a native even a single section of land was a microcosm of the continent: a cornfield, cultivated,
civilized, straight, and square, next to a stony pasture full of those
strange visitors from another planet—cows; next to that, a rolling
gully, or cattail slough, and if you were lucky, a coffee-colored river
with its dark willow, cottonwood, and boxelder grove along the bank;
then a blue-blooming flax field stretching up to meet that intimidating,
magnificent sky full of tornadoes, thunderstorms, stars clear as sword
points heading toward earth on summer nights.

Though others imagined them small, the people were sometimes
passionate and mercurial as that sky above them. I learned to love
poetry from one of those, an immigrant Icelandic carpenter named
Einar Hallgrimsson. Einar was a bachelor, inside a school only a year
or two in his life, I suppose, but nevertheless literate and well-read in
several languages and capable of turning an elegant phrase in at least
English and Icelandic.

He and my father loved to drink whiskey and argue, and as a boy
of perhaps ten, I often tagged along with them to Einar's magical
house. He built it in an alley behind the Big Store, and lined every
wallspace with bookshelves from floor to ceiling. Even in the bath-
room, you meditated at eye level with Goethe, Emerson, Icelandic
sagas, and *The National Geographic* from 1913 to 1921. Einar might
say in his old country voice, "Your father and I are going to discuss
business in the kitchen. Now you sit here in my green chair, and read
some poems. When we're done, I'll come read one for you." The
business was, of course, a pint of whiskey, satirical stories, and maybe
an argument about Republican obtuseness or Lutheran narrow-mind-
edness. When the whiskey was done, Einar lumbered back into the
living room, moved me out of his green chair, and read—perhaps
"The Shooting of Dan McGrew," a Shakespeare sonnet, Longfellow's

"Village Blacksmith," or even an old Viking poem in Icelandic. He did not discriminate among these poems, but loved them all. They were the air he breathed, and went into every wood cabinet he ever built. I met few college professors as intelligent as Einar.

A while ago, Valdimar Bjornson, an escaped and distinguished Minneota Icelander of the last generation, sent me a letter that my great uncle John Holme wrote in 1922 to Valdimar's father Gunnar, the founder of Minneota's newspaper. It is always strange to read other people's mail, even if they are dead. This conversation was probably not meant to be overheard, but in reading it, I had a weird sense, not of violating privacy, but that I had written the letter myself, and that Uncle John, or his shade, had been writing my poems for years.

He was born Gudjon Johannesson in Iceland, and emigrated with his three brothers to Minnesota. One brother, my grandfather Sveinn, homesteaded. Two went to Bellingham, Washington, grew apples and fished. John went to college, became the first educated Holm, and worked as a journalist and author. He wrote campaign biographies, magazine articles, and was regular correspondent for a New York newspaper.

In his letter, he tips off the small town editor on selling articles, reminisces about Icelanders he knows on the east coast, asks about his old girlfriend in Minneota, who (perish the thought!) married a Norwegian. Finally he discusses his current home—New York:

> *I wish I could get out of this damned town and nev-ever see it again. It is the only spot I ever struck in the United States that I don't like . . . I am going to sell out soon and move over to Jersey or some spot in Connecticut. What I want to do is buy a little farm . . . I am hankering a good deal to visit my old haunts again, especially Minneota and the old farm, and sooner or later I will get there. I have changed very little except that I*

am getting gray, and so damned old that I have begun to wear suspenders
again, but I have not yet taken to golf. I reckon that will be the next step.

He died a year or two later in Flushing, Long Island, having never seen Minneota or his old farm again. When I finished reading his 55-year-old letter, I drove eight miles north of Minneota to make sure the farm was still there.

BILL HOLM SR.

This strong, nervous, profane man loved whiskey, stories, and laughter. He had a velvety spirit, but the alligator hide of a blond man who sat on a tractor in wind and sun too long. I got dragged along with him into the Powerhouse when I was a boy, while he and Uncle Avy Snidal, with his clawed thumb, the only remains of his hand, and Einar the Mayor Hallgrimsson, and farmers from north of town sat around drinking, waiting for the combine to get fixed. He god-damned this, and god-damned that and god-damned a politician as "an asshole to dumb to piss with his pants full." Finally one of the farmers snuck down the street to the hardware store, came back with sixty-penny spikes, and Bill Holm, with grunts and "eh's" got coerced into his trick. He took out of his striped overalls pocket an old red handkerchief, full of oat dust and sweat, and wrapped it around the spike. He bent the handkerchief, turning the big nail into a perfect V. Some farmer always picked up the bent spikes that clunked to the bar and hung them together like fence links. Those souvenirs from his strong hands went home from the Minneota liquor store while I sat in amazed silence wondering at my father's power. After a while, a couple of farmers gone one whiskey over the top of the dam started arguing about the right time to sell cattle, the best soybean fertilizer, the cleanest barn. Voices rose, fists closed, moved meanly around the beer bottles. My father, who liked loud talk but hated quarrels, came up behind, locking a vise-grip hand affectionately on each neck: "Hell, boys, let's have a drink over here, I'll buy." The fight ended before it started, throttled by that spike-bending thumb pressed into a neck. What good is strength if you have to use it? That's what my father taught me without meaning to.

FRED MANFRED IN ROUNDWIND: LUVERNE, MINNESOTA

He is a tall, thin beanpole of a man, with a good shock of hair—blond or grey depending on the light falling on it. Sometimes he is over 60, sometimes in his 20s. He likes making low houses in tall places, to be higher than his own roofline, but not so high as the hill. Humility, too, should be practiced in moderation; too much of it takes the spunk and life out of a man.

But he does not talk moderately! No story is lost on him, so he rolls them around in his mouth like a good chew of snooze, occasionally spitting at the page to see how it falls, how the pattern looks. He invents books the same way he invents houses, finding a hill or a rock wall, old lumber, black meteorites, red quartz, grey granite, liberated from a farmer's bean field and hauled home in the trunk of the old Cadillac—things already there but with no shape yet. He pulls at his beard, looks around to see where they can be piled up in an orderly way, and if after piling and mortaring, you might possibly live in them with comfort and elegance. If one house is eaten by a state, a bank, or a woman, there are always more rocks in more beanfields, more hillsides to pile.

On the wall of the house, a carved board with a Frisian sentence— "Sjuch, God is great en wy begripe Him net." How does it sound in Frisian, I ask? He roars it with thunderclap consonants, sledgehammer vowels, throwing arms and fingers into the air. Suddenly he is eleven feet tall. His leap is a cross between a ballet dancer, a basketball center, and a hundred-year-old fence post coming up from hard ground on its own power. "God is great, and we can't grip him around." If you finish getting your hands on something, it is dead. That is his wisdom—why he opens his hands so much, why nothing ever gets entirely done.

RONALD

I

Town folk call Ronald the road runner. He strolls twelve miles down
the highway to Marshall, balances on the railroad tracks four miles
to Taunton, passes their doors five time a day, always going fast in
five different directions. One skinny leg in mud-caked Levis strikes
vigorously out front, pulling the back one along for fellowship. Road
running, they call it. No money, no car, too dumb to pass the test, so
Ronald walks while we drive. Though one edge of town is only a mile
from the other, there's no parking spot within two blocks of the post
office at 9:30. Cars are triple parked and running, neighborly exhaust
fumes sidling up together. Starting the Buick for two blocks to get mail
is proof of moral fiber, money in the bank, and non-residence on the
same planet as Ronald, the road runner, who walks all the way to the
post office to get the mail, which he can't read.

II

For three hot summer months, Ronald wears the same lavender, pearl-
buttoned shirt, a purple cowboy boot embroidered on each shoulder.
For me, he works days moving piles of old lumber, pulling up bur-
dock, bagging asphalt shingles. For others, he picks rock, pulls corn
out of beans, and shovels oats in a grainery. Between times, he walks.
Ten miles a day. Up and down the tracks. He sweats grandly and
ripens by August. As the lavender darkens, the boots turn black and

finally disappear and the shirt, now royal purple, begins to unravel like a used empire. Watching it, I think: this noble shirt has presence beyond itself . . . up to one hundred feet. It is the aura that vibrates around a medium's head. It has history and labor in it, the humiliation and grief felt by the poor and slow. If Ronald could read, he could write *The History of My Shirt: America in the Twentieth Century.* Instead, he waits until fall when someone buys him a new one for all the wrong reasons.

III

They taught Ronald to sweep at the slow school in Canby after giving up on reading. Now he grabs my broom like a violin, and fiddles dust entirely off the porch. Spiders scurry for shelter, boxelder bugs between planks fly away into the afternoon, a cadenza of garbage and bugs. Done, he hands me the driver's manual, says, "Can you teach me?"

"No, Ronald," I reply. "Artists like us, we take money."

IV

During the worst of the snowstorm, Ronald shovels the sidewalk. When he gets to the door, hand open to collect, the walk is already half drifted shut. I point out to him the foolishness of his enterprise: "Wait, Ronald," I say, "till the snow stops blowing. Why move the same drift, over and over, back and forth?"

"Yah," he says, looks vacant, doesn't take his hand away.

The cold almost deodorizes him, ice caking his peach fuzz, frosting his hat. Not quite. I wrinkle my nose and pay up. After he leaves, I wonder which one of us truly shovels the same drift a hundred times, or whether we all only fool ourselves about whether the storm is over, the work done.

V

Ronald ambles into the weekly paper office and stands at the counter. No-bath-for-a-month odor follows him like a bride's train, and arrives at his coat just a second later. Edna, seventy and crabby, sees him and asks, "What do you want, Ronald?"

"Can I buy some words?"

A little astounded, she says, "I think you better talk to George."

Her son comes out, waits.

"I want you to make me some words."

"What, Ronald?"

"Can you put in the paper that I don't want to talk to Craig Peterson no more and he don't have to come to my house?"

"No."

"Okay," says Ronald, grin unchanged, unchanging, cast in surgical steel on his face the day he was born. He lurches out, his train still wrinkling the air at the counter for a minute before it slinks under the door into the winter afternoon, and follows him up the street.

VI

Three-fourths asleep in that drowse where music exists but words disappear, I hear the irregular loud thump: front door banging as if a bear was swatting it. It stops: I sink again and finish Mahler's Tenth Symphony while getting rubbed by a black-haired woman. Now the kitchen door thumps. I wait. It stops. Now the south door; I see four horses charging in different directions, the snap when the body comes apart. Now the front door again. I charge up, frothing. It is Ronald, dumb grin, smelling like he just finished a swimming lesson in an old slough. "Have you got anything for me to do?"

I scream, my eyeballs bulge, a Johnstown flood of invective thunders out. I am imperious, Achilles and Hector on the battlements. Ronald is washed away, vacant, can't understand a word of it, but knows it contains murder and retreats to neutral ground. I slam the door, cracking the frame. This costs me $50. I start the nap again. No use. He will be back in half an hour, knows my car is home, and even Hitler could be softened up by a beaten dog's eyes.

VII

Ronald gawks around the living room while I rummage for money to pay him for some job I didn't need done in the first place. Surrounding him are books he can't read, keyboards he can't play, scores by composers with unpronounceable names, paintings that don't look like his visible world, and memorabilia from countries he can't find on the map. He does not look threatened by my armor, but I am by his. He's my doppelgänger: Holm after the stroke, the grief that snapped him, ten years in prison. But I am not his. The universe, like Mephistopheles, gives no gifts for which you do not sign in blood, and pay up, unexpectedly.

CATHOLICS

When I grew up, western Minnesota was organized into two pitched, sometimes warring camps—Catholics and Lutherans. They told us in Luther League that the Knights of Columbus stored guns for the coming revolution in the church basement and took oaths in blood to murder Lutheran babies who could not forcibly be converted to the true church. The Romans would presumably burn all extant copies of Luther's *Second Catechism,* thereby extinguishing the possibility of intellectual freedom and human growth. An adult Lutheran minister told these things to children who knew no better. He should not have done so. Farming land with Ezra Taft Benson in the Department of Agriculture was trouble enough, without furtive attempts to start the Thirty Years' War over again in Lyon County.

In Minneota there was a Catholic Bank and a Lutheran Bank, Catholic and Lutheran groceries, insurance, garages, and you took your business where you preferred the theology. Cross the line and there was talk about giving "them" the business. My father, a skeptic, probably an agnostic, seemed to have no truck with such policy, because he drove Catholic cars and ate Catholic hamburger. This showed considerable fearlessness and good sense that I did not appreciate sufficiently at the time.

I grew up imagining Catholics had access to mysterious sexuality and joy not available to chilly hearted Scandinavians whose pursed lips and dried souls disapproved of everything that smacked of delight, laughter, or reverence for whatever passed middle class understanding. Catholics married in mysterious and interminable ceremonies with incense, bells, and gold robes, conducted in smoky southern language no one understood. Married in the morning, they drank whiskey, ate ham, told stories through the afternoon, and finished off by hiring a band, drinking more whiskey, dancing the polka, schottische, and old time waltz all night, ending up at dawn with hugging, love-making, well-wishing, and a divine ecstatic hangover. When Lutherans married, they read St. Paul, issued warnings, drank coffee in the basement, shook hands, and went to work the next day. That, presumably, was why so many more Catholics were always getting born. Everyone said they were taking over.

After twenty years I learned something about the dark and puritan side of Catholicism. I saw it in Ireland, and then understood it better in western Minnesota. Humans travel to see their own home clearly. But as a boy, I envied Catholics what was romantic and joyful in their church. I loved midnight mass on Christmas Eve, the only respectable time for a Lutheran to be present inside Rome's brick bastions on the prairie.

THE OLD ROUND-UP SALOON

When Sister Helen preached above the Round-Up, they came clomping up that rickety staircase, those bored with mumbled Glorias, slow hymns full of tears, who longed for noise, the spirit flopping visibly around the room.

Below, pool-shooters, rummy-players, snoose-chewers and beer-drinkers barely looked up from their games; hardly a chair scratched back across the oiled floor; hardly a click missed on the ivory billiards counter strung across the ceiling; hardly a chaw spattered over the brass spittoon, as the faithful parade came upstairs to meeting.

Maybe once somebody made the remark that in this town the strong in spirit and weak in head were one and the same, and then returned to the game, slapping another card on the pile, pulling hat-brim over eye.

Upstairs Sister Helen strummed guitar, screeched Bible, and remembered languages no one ever spoke, and the feet of the faithful, full of the spirit at last, stomped those creaking boards in something resembling four/four time till, underneath, the ceiling fan slowly turning over the rummy players' hats dropped a halo of dust onto the table and sanctified their game.

Finally, the rummy players heard Sister Helen's voice rising to a shout, and with their inner eye they saw her gesture: right arm in loose white gown, bolt up to roof: "Heaven above!" Left down toward dust now settling on the rummy table: "And Hell below!" Also maybe a hallelujah or two or three at the gift of at least one kind of truth revealed and said clean.

SUNDAY MORNING

6:00 Sunday morning. I wake to grey light, hear birds. More than birds. A human voice mumbling. I get up, stumble to the kitchen. There is a naked man in the garden eating lilacs, making a noise not quite like singing. He holds onto an iron fence post, weaving, while, with his free hand, he stuffs lilacs into his mouth. He's got a Janus body, an old athlete's hind end, but the front of a Roman emperor, bloated and pendulous, now maybe from lilacs. I don't believe it. A naked man in the garden eating lilacs! I dress in half-dark and go out the front door to the neighbor's house. I see the lilac eater out of the corner of my eye. I walk softly up the neighbor's dark stairs, and wake him.

"There's a naked man in the garden eating lilacs." He rolls over, looks up with confused eyes.

"Are you writing another poem?"

"No, he's there."

He stumbles up now and we both look: "Well, I'll be damned! There's a naked man in the garden eating lilacs!"

"Yes. Who?"

"Is it Sam?"

We look. Another neighbor comes out with dog dish in one hand, dry kibble bag in the other.

"Look, Ed. There's a naked man in the garden eating lilacs."

"Huh?"

"Look."

"Well, I'll be damned!"

The naked man in the garden eating lilacs pays no attention to any of us, goes on holding the fence post, eating more lilacs.

"Well, we'd better do something."

We close in.

"Is it Sam?"

"No. I don't know."

Hard to recognize a man naked with his mouth full of lilacs. We get closer. The mumbling turns into language. "God, the Father." Lilac. "God, the Son." Another lilac. "God, the Holy Ghost." Another lilac, another weave.

"Pretty cold here, Sam, better put your pants on."

His pants lie in a heap on the gravel.

"Want my pants?" Lilac. "God is here." Lilac. "Told me to eat." Weave, lilac.

"Cold out here, Sam, almost winter."

"Not cold where I'm going in hell." Lilac.

His mouth is stuffed so full of lilac leaves his lips swell out. He talks through this green mush of lilacs, a few strands of soggy leaves hanging down, words wet and muffled.

"I been a bad boy. God told me to do this. His son's dead. What the hell kind of a deal is that? See him! There he is! Back of the tree! God, the Father. God, the Son. Think it's cold now? Wait till you see what I do when I get this post out. God, the Father. God, the Son."

I see an anchor tattoo on the arm holding the fence post, and two small tattooed words, one on each breast. I can't read the two words that weave back and forth between gulps of lilac.

"I don't think he's drunk. We'd better get his wife."

We walk the few blocks, knock on the dark door. She is dressed.

"Better come get Sam. He's naked in the garden eating lilacs."

She is not astounded. "He's been drinking two weeks, just quit, got out of bed at 2:30 in the morning. I'll have to call the boys and take him to Willmar."

We make a silent procession through the grey light. He's still there, weaving, mumbling, eating lilacs.

"Come on, Sam, get your pants on now, and we'll go for a nice ride today."

She is gentle with him, motherly, not angry but sighing. He goes on eating lilacs, mouth stuffed full, his mumbling mushier now.

"God, he told me. The father."

"Spit that out, Sam. You'll get sick."

She hands him his pants. Now he looks small, naked, pathetic, penis shriveled in the cold, belly bloated like a baby's, too big for his skinny legs.

"Spit it out." She pulls his head down, opens his mouth. As a wet lilac glob falls out into the grass, he reaches over for another leaf.

"God . . ."

She pulls his hand away calmly. "No. Enough."

He stuffed in so many that he can't get them all out, and slaps his own cheek. She pulls out a wet lilac chunk, as if reaching in to get matted hay that clogged a baler. With his pants on, he is over fifty again, but she is still his mother.

"Come on home now."

He stops stubbornly midway out of the yard and fixes her with his eye: "How come you've got more authority than God?"

She says nothing, takes him by the arm down the street. When they're gone, I walk back, hang onto the fence post a minute, stare at the half-bare lilac branches, a few white blossoms still flavoring the air with their smell.

Was I only dreaming a poem when I saw the naked man in my

garden eating lilacs in the grey Sunday morning light? No, the real poem eats lilacs every Sunday morning, under steeples, with crosses, mumbles over coffins, waters the bellies of babies, legs too rubbery to run away from the green mush given us to eat. This tattooed eye-chart on legs weaves back and forth in front of the lilac altar so that we can't make out the true words. Church bells ring now all through town, rising over bird cries, the naked man in the garden eating lilacs riding down the long highway to Willmar and sleep.

SINGING LATIN IN NEW ULM

When north Europe's cast-offs moved to Minnesota, they left some baggage behind. The Germans didn't move Goethe, or the Poles Chopin; the Danes forgot Holberg, and the Swedes did not invite Strindberg to join them here. But they brought both their religions with new ferocity in them further from the sea, and the rudiments of their old country church architecture. In western Minnesota brick is Catholic, wood is Lutheran. Tiny bare frame churches contain Norwegians or Icelanders, but anything with a dome, spires, ornamental glass, and stone is likely to be full of Poles or Germans. Thus New Ulm, like its European namesake, is a cathedral town.

On a sunny Sunday afternoon in mid-winter, the Prairie Chorale sings its Christmas concert in that old cathedral. Harsh light goldens the stone, brightening up dim corners in the big vaulted room. Like all stone interiors, this is full of echos that magnify the smallest sound many times beyond itself. As the audience grows, there rises a steady buzz of shuffling overshoes, scratching wool, squishing goose-down, muffled whispering that's like an undertone of oversized out-of-season crickets. Medieval cathedrals must have been like this too—never silent, a single sneeze resounding like a gunshot or a helicopter rising.

The singers process; the buzz diminuendos; two hundred folded programs do not open simultaneously. The concert begins with a Pachelbel *Magnificat*.

Magnificat anima mea Dominum.
Et exultavit spiritus meus in Deo salutari meo.

The counterpoint threads onward toward the phrase that ended almost everything sung or said inside churches like this for thousands of years:

Gloria Patri, et Filio, Et Spiritui Sancto.
Sicut Erat in principio, et nunc, et semper,
et in saecula saeculorum, Amen.

The Chorale performs decently. Singing in a stone bowl clearly delights them, and they stand listening for ten seconds after the piece to the ghost of their own voices saying *Amen* all over the room. Under it, as everyone there understands whether conscious of it or not, is the ghost of that *Gloria* in Chartres, Cologne, York Minster, Norwegian stave churches, St. Peter's and St. Paul's, and old Ulm itself. The ghost of Europe, uncomfortable in this Midwest winter light, does its best to remain beautiful and intelligent.

The singers peer out over a lake of faces swimming in the ancient noise of that music. The front row is most beautiful: a line of old priests, white hair rising over white collars, pink wrinkles between, suits black as whale bodies. Not one of those priests seems likely to see eighty again, and you imagine them alive at the foundation of the world, black and white and ancient even then. They weep while they smile! The mightiest weeping of all comes from the chief priest sitting on the aisle.

After some Christmas carols, the director turns and announces to the audience that four *Ave Marias* will be sung, and that it is appropriate to do this since today is the Feast of the Immaculate Conception.

Ancestors of almost everyone in the room were persecuted or killed depending on whether or not they entertained this particular theological idea, but the young blond director does not mention this, nor should he. This is Minnesota, an afternoon for rejoicing of heart.

Four *Aves* come: an ancient plain song; austere counterpoint from the Renaissance; a romantic Russian setting; finally, a dissonant one composed by an American. Four times those words return, always the same, whatever the notes that embroider them.

> *Ave Maria, gratia plena,*
> *Dominus tecum.*
> *Benedicta tu in mulieribus,*
> *Et benedictus fructus ventris tui, Jesus.*
> *Sancta Maria, Mater Dei,*
> *Ora pro nobis peccatoribus,*
> *Nunc et in hora mortis nostrae.*

The joyful weeping from the old priests, huge tears of praise streaming down the wrinkled creek beds on their cheeks, now overwhelms the singers too, and the afternoon continues as if magically presided over by the Virgin herself who heard her name called four times and appeared as an invisible presence under the stone vaulting. The music now sounds that forgiveness often spoken about in rooms like this. Something female softens the prairies today, maybe even, for one afternoon, America.

At the end of the concert, more Latin, perhaps the greatest sentence of all:

> *O magnum mysterium,*
> *et admirable sacramentum,*
> *Ut animalia viderent Dominum natum . . .*

What a great mystery that animals should see a God born! And yet, who else would notice it? Men, busy with practical missiles and fertilizers have to be worked on by magic before they stop their quarrels long enough to watch and listen with any openness of heart or intelligence.

"Silent Night" in German with a guitar, and then the singers recess to the basement to smoke, compliment each other, get into street clothes, and drive on to another concert. Magic cannot last too long or it loses power; Beethoven broke the spell cast by his dreamy improvisations with harsh banged chords.

But it continues a little while. The singers stop buzzing suddenly; a presence enters the basement, the beautiful old chief priest who sat on the aisle staunches his tears while hugging the director. He speaks:

"I was bishop of this diocese for thirty years, have been in this cathedral church my whole life as a priest, and I have never heard anything so beautiful as the great gift of music you gave this afternoon. And your Latin! It is so wonderful to hear Latin again after all these years; and you sing it so clearly, so correctly, with such feeling, and . . ." he pauses, and a sad shadow passes over his moist face, "I suppose . . ." he is almost choking, "you are all," another burst of tears, "Protestants."

Protestants! Indeed they are. O magnum mysterium. . . .

THE MUSIC OF FAILURE:
VARIATIONS ON AN IDEA

PRELUDE, THE THEME FOR THE VARIATIONS

The ground bass is failure; America is the key signature; Pauline Bardal is the lyrical tune that sings at the center; Minneota, Minnesota, is the staff on which the tunes are written; poverty, loneliness, alcoholism, greed, disease, insanity, war, and spiritual and political emptiness are the tempo markings; Walt Whitman and this sentence from the *Bhagavad-Gita* are the directions for expression:

> *Die, and you win heaven. Conquer, and you enjoy the earth. Stand up now . . . and resolve to fight. Realize that pleasure and pain, gain and loss, victory and defeat, are all one and the same: then go into battle. Do this and you cannot commit any sin.*

The true subject, the melody that counterpoints everything but is never heard, like Elgar's secret theme for the *"Enigma Variations,"* is my own life, and yours, and how they flow together to make the life of a community, and then a country, and then a world.

ANOTHER IDEA FROM WALT WHITMAN THAT
NO ONE WANTS TO HEAR

At fifteen, I could define failure fast: to die in Minneota, Minnesota. Substitute any small town in Pennsylvania, or Nebraska, or Bulgaria,

and the definition held. To be an American meant to move, rise out
of a mean life, make yourself new. Hadn't my own grandfathers
transcended Iceland, learned at least some English, and died with a
quarter section free and clear? No, I would die a famous author, a distinguished and respected professor at an old university, surrounded by
beautiful women, witty talk, fine whiskey, Mozart. There were times
at fifteen, when I would have settled for central heat and less Jell-O,
but I kept my mental eye on the "big picture."

Later, teaching Walt Whitman in school, I noticed that my students did not respond with fervor to the lines,

> *With music strong I come, with my cornets and my drums,*
> *I play not marches for accepted victors only, I play marches for conquer'd*
> *   and slain persons.*

> *Have you heard that it was good to gain the day?*
> *I also say it is good to fall, battles are lost in the same spirit in which they*
> *   are won.*

> *I beat and pound for the dead,*
> *I blow through my embouchures my loudest and gayest for them.*

> *Vivas to those who have fail'd!*
> *And to those war-vessels sunk in the sea!*
> *And to those themselves who sank in the sea!*
> *And to all generals that lost engagements, and all overcome heroes!*
> *And to the numberless unknown heroes equal to the greatest heroes known!*

I left Minneota at the beginning of America's only lost war. While
I traveled, got educated, married, divorced, and worldly, the national

process of losing went on: a president or two shot, an economy collapsed, a man whom every mother in America warned every child against accepting rides or candy from, was in the flesh overwhelmingly elected president, and then drummed into luxurious disgrace for doing the very things those mothers warned against. The water underneath America turned out to be poisoned. Cities like Denver, Los Angeles, Chicago were invisible under air that necessitated warning notices in the newspaper. A rumor flourished that the Arabs bought the entire Crazy Mountains in Montana. Oil gurgled onto gulls' backs north of San Francisco. The war finally ended in disgrace, the Secretary of State mired as deep in lies as Iago. America, the realized dream of the eighteenth-century European Enlightenment, seemed to have sunk into playing out a Shakespearean tragedy, or perhaps a black comedy.

Yet as history brought us failure, it brought us no wisdom. The country wanted as little as my students to hear those lines from *Leaves of Grass*. It was not "good to fall," not good to be "sunk in the sea," not good to be among the "numberless unknown heroes." We elected, in fact, a famous actor to whom failure was incomprehensible as history itself, a man who responded to visible failure around him by ignoring it and cracking hollow jokes.

In the meantime, I aged from twenty to forty, found myself for all practical purposes a failure, and settled almost contentedly back into the same rural town which I tried so fiercely to escape. I could not help noticing that personal and professional failure were not my private bailiwick. I knew almost no one still on their first marriage. Friends, too, were short of money and doing work that at twenty they would have thought demeaning or tedious. Children were not such an unpremeditated joy as maiden aunts led us to expect, and for the precocious middle-aged, health and physical beauty had begun to fail. It looked, as the old cliché had it, as if we were going to die after all, and the procedure would not be quite so character-building as the *Reader's Digest* and the Lutheran minister implied.

Heard from inside, the music of failure sounded not the loudest, gayest marches for cornets and drums, but a melancholy cello, strings slowly loosening, melody growing flaccid, receding toward silence. The country closed its ears against the tune; citizens denied that they had ever heard it. "Tomorrow," they said, but this was only another way of saying "yesterday," which did not exist quite as they imagined it. This continual denial gave a hollow, whining quality to conversations. Discussions of politics, work, or marriage sounded like a buzzsaw speaking English.

The first settlers of America imagined paradise, God's city made visible on earth. Grand rhetoric for a pregnancy, it was, like all births, bloodier and messier than anyone imagined at the moment of conception. English Puritans who came to build a just and godly order began by trying to exterminate Indian tribes. They tried to revise the English class system of rich landowners and poor yeomen by sharing a common bounty, but this lasted only until somebody realized that true profit lay in landowning, here as in England. The same settlers who declared with Proudhon that "property is theft" wound up working as real estate agents. Old European habits of success died hard.

Hypocrisy is not unusual in human history; it is the order of the day. What has always been unusual in the United States is the high-toned rhetoric that accompanied our behavior, our fine honing of the art of sweeping contradictions under the rug with our eternal blank optimism. But if we examined, without sentimentality, the failures and contradictions of our own history, it would damage beyond repair the power of that public rhetoric, would remove the arch-brick from the structure of the false self we have built for ourselves, in Minneota as elsewhere.

I labored under the weight of that rhetoric as a boy, and when I am tired now, I labor under it still. It is the language of football, a successful high school life, earnest striving and deliberate ignoring, money, false cheerfulness, mumbling about weather. Its music is composed by the radio, commercials for helpful banks and deodorants breathing out at you between stanzas. In cities now, ghetto blasters play it at you in the street; you are serenaded by tiny orchestras hidden in elevators or in rafters above discount stores. It is the music of tomorrow and tomorrow and tomorrow. It is not what Whitman had in mind by beating and pounding for the dead. True dead, unlike false dead, hear what we sing to them.

THE MUSIC OF EXPERIENCE; THE NOISE OF FAILURE

Years ago, I traveled to Waterton, Alberta, the north end of Glacier Park, and spent a whole sunny, windy August afternoon sitting on a slope high in the mountains listening to an Aspen tree. I wrote a small poem about that experience:

> *Above me, wind does its best*
> *to blow leaves off the Aspen*
> *tree a month too soon. No use,*
> *wind, all you succeed in doing*
> *is making music, the noise*
> *of failure growing beautiful.*

I did not understand my own poem at the time.

As a small boy, I sang loudly, clearly, and as elderly ladies told me, wonderfully. I knew better, but knowledge didn't interfere with love (as it so often doesn't), and music remained the true channel to the deepest part of my feeling life. Happiness (or at least emotion) could be described by notes with stems, and the noises of the inner life made audible by reading and sounding those marks. Though never so skilled a musician as to have made a genuine living from it, I was skilled enough to know precisely the deficiencies of every performance I ever gave. Perfection was not a gift given to many in music. Mozart may have had it. I did not.

In an odd way, this melancholy knowledge of my own musical imperfection goes on teaching me something about the wholesomeness of failure every day of my adult life. I have sometimes, like the United States, been too obtuse to remember it, but then I hear again the noise of aspen leaves.

PAULINE BARDAL AT THE PIANO

I first heard a piano in the back room of Peterson's farmhouse, three miles east of my father's place. An only child, too young and disinterested to do any real work, I was left indoors while my father was out giving Wilbur a hand with some chore, probably splitting a half-pint to make the job more pleasant. Wilbur was a bachelor, but kept his aged father, Steve, and a sort of combination housekeeper and nurse, Pauline Bardal, to look after both of them. Pauline was born in 1895 to the first generation of Icelandic immigrants in western Minnesota. When I knew her in the late forties or early fifties, she must have been nearing sixty. Age is relative to children, so I did not think of her as being particularly old. She was simply Pauline, and would remain that way until she died thirty years later.

She was almost six feet tall, without a bit of fat on her, and this made her bones visible, particularly in the hands, joints moving with large gestures as if each finger had reasoning power of its own. Her leanness was partly genetic, but partly also the result of continual work. In the cities she would have been called a domestic, though her duties at Peterson's and elsewhere always involved nursing the infirm and dying. In Minneota's more informal class labeling, she was simply Pauline.

After finishing her duties with bread, chickens, or tending to old Steve, Pauline retired to the den for a half hour of music. I was invited to listen and always delighted by the prospect. She sat herself on the bench, arranging her bones with great dignity and formality. Music was not a trifling matter even if your hands were fresh from flour bin or hen house. Pauline did not play light music; though she was conventionally religious in a Lutheran sort of way, I knew, even as a child, that music was her true spiritual exercise. She always played slowly, and I suppose, badly, but it made no difference. She transported both herself and me by the simple act of playing. Her favorite pieces were Handel's "Largo" from *Xerxes,* and a piano arrangement of the finale of Bach's *St. Matthew Passion:* "In Deepest Grief." She had never learned true fingering, and got most of her musical experience at an old pump organ that she played for church services. She did not so much strike the keys as slide with painstaking slowness from one to the next, leaving sufficient time for the manual rearrangement of the bones in her hands. This gave all her performances a certain halting dignity, even if sometimes questionable accuracy. It was always said around Minneota that her most moving performances were at funerals, where enormously slow tempos seemed appropriate. She played the sad Bach as a postlude while mourners filed past the open coffin for the last time.

But Pauline at the keyboard was not a lugubrious spirit. Watching that joy on her bony face as her fingers slid over the yellowed keyboard of the old upright, it became clear to me even as a child that neither her nor my true life came from kneading bread or candling eggs or fluffing pillows in a sick bed, but happened in the presence of those noises, badly as they might be made by your own hands. They lived in the inner lines of that Bach, so difficult to manage cleanly with work-stiffened fingers. You felt Bach's grandeur moving under you at whatever speed. The Handel "Largo," though it has become something of a joke for sophisticated listeners through its endless bad piano transcriptions is, in fact, a glorious piece, one of the great gifts from Europe. Even on farms in rural Minnesota, you deserve the extraordinary joy of hearing it for the first time, as if composed in your presence, only for you. I heard it that way, under Pauline's hands. The Minneapolis Symphony playing Beethoven's *Ninth* in the living room could not have been so moving or wonderful as that "Largo" in Peterson's back room.

Pauline, in American terms, was a great failure: always poor, never married, living in a shabby small house when not installed in others' back rooms, worked as a domestic servant, formally uneducated, English spoken with the odd inflections of those who learn it as a second language, gawky and not physically beautiful, a badly trained musician whose performances would have caused laughter in the cities. She owned nothing valuable, traveled little, and died alone, the last of her family. If there were love affairs, no one will now know anything about them, and everyone involved is surely dead. Probably she died a virgin, the second most terrible fate, after dying broke, that can befall an American.

But, as the scripture bids, "Let us now praise famous men," and I mean to praise not merely Pauline, but her whole failed family, and through them the music of failure in America.

THE HISTORY OF A FAILED IMMIGRANT

Minneota is a community born out of failure about 1880. By that I mean that no one ever arrived in Minneota after being a success elsewhere. It is an immigrant town, settled by European refuse, first those starved out of Ireland, then Norway, Iceland, Sweden, Holland, Belgium. Given the harshness of western Minnesota's climate and landscape, people did not come to retire or loaf. They came to farm, and had they been successful at it in the old world, would not have uprooted their families, thrown away culture and language, and braved mosquitoes and blizzards for mere pleasure. Minneota is, of course, a paradigm for the settling of the whole country. We are a nation of failures who have done all right and been lucky. Perhaps it is some ancient dark fear of repeating our own grandfathers' lives that makes us reluctant to acknowledge failure in national or private life.

Pauline's father, Frithgeir, came in 1880 in the third wave of nationalities to Minneota: the Icelanders. He likely read one of the pamphlets circulated by the American government in all Scandinavian countries, describing free and fertile land available on the Great Plains for farmers of sturdy, sufficiently Caucasian stock. The United States was always particular about the race of its failures. The pamphlet probably mentioned glowingly the bountiful harvests, rich topsoil, good drainage and pasturage, cheap rail transport, and healthful brac-ing climate. Frithgeir Joakimsson, who took his new last name, Bardal, from his home valley in north Iceland, arrived in 1880, found most of the best land gone, and picked perhaps the hilliest, stoniest, barest though loveliest farm acreage in that part of western Minnesota.

He was thirty-seven years old, single, and, in all likelihood, knew not a word of English when he came. Pauline, when she was old, dis-posed of her family's books to good homes, and gave me her father's first English grammar and phrase book that she said he used on the boat. It was in Danish, English, and Icelandic, well-worn though intact. Pauline clearly treasured it. Leafing through it now, I imagine rough farmer's hands, something like Pauline's, holding the book on an open deck in mid-Atlantic, sea wind rustling the pages under his thumb— *"Hvar er vegurinn vestur till Minneota?"*

For the first five years, Frithgeir farmed alone. Probably he raised sheep and hay, the only things an Icelandic farmer knew. In 1886, at age forty-three, he married Guthlaug Jonsdottir, a new immigrant whose family came from the wildest, most remote fjord in east Iceland, Borgarfjord, ringed with blood-red liparite mountains and precipitous scree slopes. Already thirty-five then, she was pregnant five times between 1887 and 1895 when Pauline, the last daughter, was born. One son, Pall, died an infant in 1889. Four out of five children alive was a lucky percentage then. But Frithgeir's luck did not hold for long in the new world. I give his obituary in its entirety, as I found it on a yellow, brittle page of the *Minneota Mascot* for Friday, September 8, 1899:

Last Saturday, while F. J. Bardal was mowing hay on his farm in Lincoln Co., the horses made a sudden start, jerking the mower which happened at that time to be on the slope of a hill, so that Mr. Bardal fell from his machine. His leg was caught in a wheel and he was dragged that way for a while until the horses stopped. The leg was broken above the knee and other injuries were sustained. Mr. Bardal managed to get on the mower and drive home. Dr. Thordason was sent for. He hurried out, set the bone and did all that could be done for the unfortunate man. But the injuries proved to be so serious that Mr. Bardal died last Monday morning. The funeral took place last Wednesday from the new Icelandic church in Lincoln County, Rev. B. B. Jonsson officiating.

F. Bardal was born January 13, 1843 in Bardardal Thingeyarsysla, Iceland and came to this country in 1880 and settled on his farm in

Lincoln County. He leaves a wife, three children and a stepdaughter.

Mr. Bardal was a much liked man in the community, an active member in his church, and a general favorite among his neighbors.

Done in by his own farm. He had found the only lovely hills in a flat country, but they killed him; his widow (who knew at best minimal English), was left with four children between four and twelve years old, and the poorest farm in the county. Nineteen years in the new world.

THE FURTHER HISTORY OF THREE CHILDREN, ALL FAILED

Perhaps a few genealogical books in Icelandic libraries, or some distant relative might provide a bit more history of the Bardals, but not much . . . and this is after a single century in the most information-rich country on earth! It is amazing to me sometimes how little basis we have as humans on which to remember Pericles, Augustine, Charlemagne, or for that matter, Abraham Lincoln.

Four children reached adulthood. One married and left Minneota. Guthlaug, the widow, remained on the farm till she lost it in 1937, another victim of the Great Depression. She was then a very old lady and, as local report had it, not entirely in her right mind. She died in 1943, bedridden in her little house, ninety-two years old, fifty-seven years in America.

There were three Bardals left when I was a boy: Gunnar, the oldest brother, gaunt, melancholy, silent; Rose, the middle sister, not quite right in the head, with a sideways cast to her eye, as if she saw the world from a different angle than normal people, mouth half smiling, but the unsmiling half colored by something dark and unknown; finally,

Pauline, their custodian, housekeeper, surrogate mother and father. The three trooped every Sunday morning to the old wood frame Icelandic church a block from their small house, and ascended the creaky choir loft stairs. Pauline played for services every other Sunday, and sang when she did not play.

The choir at St. Paul's Lutheran consisted of perhaps ten to fifteen elderly Icelandic ladies, mostly unmarried and immensely dignified. They formed the foundation of singing. Only three men joined them: Gunnar, a thin cavernous bass, another equally thin but raspier baritone, and me, a small fat boy of eleven or twelve who sang soprano or tenor, depending on his semi-changed voice. I was generally the single member of St. Paul's choir under seventy.

I sat by Gunnar who seemed always contemplating some indefinable sadness about which nothing could be done. His voice sounded octaves below everyday life, as if it came from a well bottom. He wore a brown, itchy, wool suit, decades out of style.

Crazy Rose sat close to Pauline. After Rose's death, when I was a teenager, I heard stories of her madness, her religious mania, wandering off to preach in Icelandic in the cornfields, but as a little boy, she seemed only Rose to me, and within the range of possible normality for adults. Children judge each other harshly, but don't make nice distinctions among the grown. Sane or mad, pillar or rake, drunk or sober, adults seem merely themselves, distinguished more by age than by variations of habit, character, or physiognomy.

Rose looked like a bird ordered to continue eating despite an interesting ruckus going on in the next nest. She pecked toward the floor a few times, not paying much attention to the kernels at her feet, then raised her beak to glance furtively around, the half smile breaking on her lips, as if what she saw was almost funny. Her face was small and thin, eyes pale and watery, almost without irises.

Rose died in 1956, in her sixties, of an embolism. Whatever was frail in the architecture of her cerebral arteries collapsed at last. Gunnar died in 1961 at seventy-four. I sang at both their funerals, and though I have no recollection of what the hymns might have been, they were surely sad and heavy-footed, perhaps *"Come Ye Disconsolate"* or the Icelandic hymn *"Just as the Flower Withers,"* or *"Abide with Me."* Hymn singing seemed one kind of preparation for the last great mysterious failure—the funeral, when the saddest and noblest of church tunes could be done with their proper gravity.

Pauline, now alone in her little house with all the family bric-a-brac piled around her, had no one to attend to, and a social security check to keep her from having to attend others for money. Yet her habits were too strong, and having worked for fifty or sixty years, she could not stop. Now she dispensed munificence like a queen. She cared for the dying and the horribly ill with no fuss, as if she were born to it. She was a one-woman hospice movement.

She once fried steaks in a farmers' night club out in the country, an odd job for a teetotaler, and for this she was probably paid a pittance. My mother tended the bar, and the two of them often drove out together. I saw them at work once; in the middle of loud country music and boisterous drinking, they tended these rough farmers, not like hired help, but like indulgent great aunts looking benevolently after children having a good time. Pauline owned an old Ford which she drove with enthusiasm. Well into her eighties she took friends on vacation and shopping trips, and made lunch runs for the senior citizens. Speaking of people sometimes ten or twenty years her junior, she said, "They're getting old, you know, and it's hard for them to get around." Pauline's gifts to me included not only music. She tended both my parents at their death beds, and when my mother, a week before she died, lost her second language, English, and spoke to me

only in her first, Icelandic, which I did not understand, Pauline translated. The gifts of the unschooled are often those we did not know we
would need—the right words, the right music.

Eternal though she seemed to me, age caught her. The end began
with the trembling hands of Parkinson's disease, a cruel irony for a
woman who took her delight in playing music, however badly. After
Gunnar and Rose died, she had a bit more money, and made room in
the old house by turning the spare bedrooms into storerooms. She
bought a used church organ, a monster from the forties that crowded
her tiny living room with speakers, pedal boards, and a gigantic brown
console. The organ seemed larger and heavier than the house itself, as
if even a tornado couldn't have budged it off the worn carpet. I once
asked what she was playing; she looked at me sadly: "See these hands,
how shaky? I can't even keep them on the keys anymore. They just
shake off . . ." Soon after this she went into the nursing home, and died
not long after, still peeved with the universe, I think, for taking music
away from her at the end. I don't even know who was there to tend her
bedside at the last. Probably she had had enough of that, and wanted
to be alone. Indeed, the solitariness of her whole life prepared her for
it. This was 1981, 101 years after her father left Thingeyarsysla for a
new life. She had lived in America eighty-six years.

MUSIC FOR AN OLD PUMP ORGAN

Pauline was buried among the Bardals in the graveyard next to the
Icelandic country church in Lincoln County. In 1922, Pauline picked
out the congregation's new reed organ, and played it for services there
for almost forty years, until the church, a victim of rural urbaniza-
tion and of Icelanders who refused to reproduce or stay on the farm,
closed its doors for lack of business. While a few miles to the west,
the Poles sensibly planted their Catholic Church in a hollow protected

from the wind, the Icelanders defied Minnesota by building on a rise in the only ridge of hills on that flat prairie. On even a calm day at that wind-swept knoll, the church windows rattled, shingles flapped, and the black granite gravestones seemed to wobble.

Pauline and I drove out to that church a few years before her death. She carried a shopping bag full of flowers and rat poison. She had a key for the back door of the church and we went up through the minister's dressing room into the sanctuary. The room, carpentered in good oak, was furnished only with chairs, pews, organ, pulpit, and the simple altar crowned by a wood cross; no statues, paintings, bric-a-brac—nothing but that wood, goldened by afternoon light from the pale yellow windows. Wind seemed to come up from inside the church, whooshing over the fine dust that covered everything. "Nobody's cleaned it since last year. It's a shame," Pauline muttered, then went to work. First, she arranged her long legs on the organ bench, carefully folding them between two wooden knee guards below the keyboard. Thus constricted, she pumped, and while checking the stops with one hand, slid over the keys with the other, playing the chords from Handel's "Largo." "The mice have not eaten the bellows," she announced with satisfaction, then launched into an old hymn with both hands. We played for each other for a while, Pauline marveling at my clean fingering. She knew, I think, that she had some responsibility for my love of playing, and was proud of herself, and of me, but it was not the sort of thing Icelanders discussed openly with each other. Skill could be remarked on, but the heart was private, and disliked language.

When we finished, she swept up the old poison in a newspaper, opened her yellow skull-and-crossboned boxes, and laid down a fresh lunch for any rodents who might presume to make a meal of God's own organ bellows. Even though the church would never likely be opened, nor the organ publicly played there again, such things ought to be attended to for their own sake. Who knew? Perhaps the dead a few feet away liked an occasional sad tune, and didn't fancy the idea of rats interfering with their music?

Pauline locked the church carefully, looking back at it with a sort of melancholy nostalgia. She proceeded to the graveyard with the rest of the contents of her shopping bag, and there performed her next errand. She swept off the graves, then put a flower or two on all of them. The row read:

Pall	Fridgeir	Gudlaug
7/25–8/2 '89	1843–1899	1851–1943
Rose		Gunnar
1890–1956		1887–1961

"And I will be between Rose and Gunnar" she said, "in not too long."

Indeed, within a few years the row was full; six dead in the graveyard of a dead church, no progeny, no empire following them, only the dry wind of a new world which promised them and all of us so much.

PACK RAT HOUSES, AND WHAT THEY TELL

The opening of the Bardal house was not greeted with amazement and that is, in itself, amazing. Traditionally in Minneota, as in villages all across the world, pack rats, generally unmarried, die in houses stuffed to the ceiling with moldy newspapers, rusted coffee cans full of money, and an overpopulation of bored cats.

The first astonishing fact about the house was the sheer amount inside it. Though tiny, it held the combined goods for a family of six

who threw nothing away. It was neither dirty, nor disorderly. The
piles had been dusted, and the narrow crevices between them vacu-
umed and scrubbed, but within some mounds, nothing had moved for
forty years. Papers were stacked neatly in order, probably put there
the week they arrived, from 1937 onward. The Bardals were schooled
historically and genetically by a thousand years of Icelandic poverty
of the meanest, most abject variety. They moved to a poor farm in the
poorest county of Minnesota, and when the Depression reduced pen-
ury to catastrophe, moved into a poor, small house in Minneota. While
their storage space shrank, their goods expanded, and the double beds
became single beds after the floor space filled up to the bedsprings.
They were a family on whom nothing was lost, not even the useless
doodads that arrived from answering every "free special offer" ad for
over a half century.

They accumulated no cans full of bank notes, no hidden treasure,
nothing of any genuine monetary value; the Bardals were, in that
regard, truly poor. But not poor in mind or spirit! They owned books
in three or four languages: Plato, Homer, Bjornsson in Norwegian,
Snorri Sturlasson in Icelandic, Whitman, Darwin, Dickens, Ingersoll,
Elbert Hubbard; piles of scores by Handel, Bach, Mozart, George
Beverly Shea, and Bjorgvin Gudmundsson; old cylinders of Caruso,
Galla-Curci, Schumann-Heink, John McCormack; cheap books
reproducing paintings and sculpture from great European museums;
organ, piano, violin, trumpet; manuals for gardening, cooking, and
home remedies; the best magazines of political commentary and art
criticism next to *Capper's Farmer,* the *Minneota Mascot,* and the *Plain
Truth;* dictionaries and grammars in three or four languages; books of
scientific marvels; Richard Burton's travel adventures; old text books
for speech and mathematics; Bibles and hymn books in every Scandinavian language, *Faust, The Reader's Digest,* and *"Sweet Hour of*

Prayer." That tiny house was a spaceship stocked to leave the planet after collecting the best we have done for each other for the last four thousand years of human consciousness. And none of it worth ten cents in the real world of free enterprise! The executors might as well have torched the house, thus saving the labor of sorting it, giving mementos to friends and peddling the rest at a garage sale on a sweltering summer afternoon. What one realized with genuine astonishment was that the Bardals piled this extraordinary junk not only inside their cramped house; that house was a metaphor for their interior life which they stocked with the greatest beauty and intelligence they understood. They read the books, played the instruments, carried the contents of that house in their heads, and took it off with them at last into their neat row in the Lincoln County graveyard.

But not entirely.... Anyone who carries a whole civilization around inside gives it to everyone they meet in conversations and public acts. Pauline gave me music; Gunnar, the model of a man who read and thought; literally, he gave me a first edition of Arthur Waley, Epictetus, and the *Heimskringla;* and Rose, in her odd way, her crazed longing for God. Not one of them had so much as a high school diploma. They gave what teachers hired for it so often fail to give.

THE IDEA OF FAILURE NOTED IN LITERATURE, BOTH OLD AND NEW

Having introduced you to Pauline and the rest of the Bardals, I reiterate the question I posed at the beginning of this essay. What is failure, and what is its use in our lives, either as private humans resident in our own Minneota of the soul, or as Americans, public citizens of the richest, most successful nation in history?

At the beginning of human consciousness, men seem not to have appreciated the virtues of failure either. The *Gilgamesh* epic, at least a thousand years older than Homer or Genesis, and thus the first record of what troubled us as humans, contains the following scene: Gilgamesh, the king, is unhappy in his willful solitude, satisfying his sexual whims, living a materially splendid life, and thoughtlessly brutalizing his subjects, yet feeling a part of himself missing. One night he wakes from a disturbing dream which he tells his mother Ninsun, a goddess, who has power to read dream symbols:

> *I saw a star*
> *Fall from the sky, and the people*
> *Of Uruk stood around and admired it,*
> *And I was zealous and tried to carry it away*
> *But I was too weak and I failed.*
> *What does it mean? I have not dreamed*
> *Like this before.*

She explains that the star symbolizes his equal—something too heavy which he will "try to lift and drive away, and fail." This worries Gilgamesh:

> *But I have never failed before, he interrupted*
> *Her, surprised himself at his anxiety.*
> *It will be a person, she continued . . .*
> *A companion who is your equal*
> *In strength, a person loyal to a friend*
> *Who will not forsake you and whom you*
> *Will never wish to leave.*

Gilgamesh thinks this over quietly, and soon after dreams again, this time of an ax: "When I tried to lift it, I failed." She consoles him:

> *This ax is a man*
> *Who is your friend and equal.*
> *He will come.*

Enkidu comes, Gilgamesh falls from godly solitude into friendship, and when Enkidu dies, falls again through grief into true humanity. The failure that so disturbs his dreams is, in fact, the longing for full consciousness as a human, and this is learned when "A man sees death in things. That is what it is to be a man." Only by failure can Gilgamesh find this wisdom, and before he does, the whole country suffers from his thoughtlessness. There is surely a lesson here, even thousands of years later, for countries that insist on denying it and being led by those who have never gone through the failure and grief necessary to see this "death in things."

Forty or fifty centuries after *Gilgamesh,* E. M. Forster imagined a similar scene in *A Passage to India,* though now there is no Enkidu to come. Mrs. Moore and her thick-headed boy, Ronny, a British civil servant, are arguing about the behavior of the English in India. Ronny trots out the clichés about God's work and the white man's burden, but his mother surveys him with an ironic eye:

> His words without his voice might have impressed her, but when she heard the self-satisfied lilt of them, when she saw the mouth moving so complacently and competently beneath the little red nose, she felt, quite illogically, that this was the not the last word on India. One touch of regret—not the canny substitute, but the true regret from the heart—would have made him a different man, and the British Empire a different institution.

The argument goes on, not a trace of regret penetrating into Ronny.

Finally, exasperated, she says,

> The desire to behave pleasantly satisfies God. . . . I think everyone fails,
> but there are so many kinds of failure. Good will and more good will
> and more good will.

Forster's point, like that of the *Gilgamesh* poet, is that human beings
learn good will by coming to a consciousness of the "death in things,"
the failure that moves Whitman to praise, and so disgusts and terrifies
us as a culture.

A FORTISSIMO BLAST FROM WALT WHITMAN, SWELLED BY THE AUTHOR'S INDIGNATION

I try, again and again, through literature, music, history, and experience, to get at the point of failure—but I fail. Perhaps that *is* my
point. Clear logical structures, much as I love them myself, are not so
germane as the "touch of regret that comes from the heart" in understanding what I am trying to penetrate.

This idea began with an image, a comparison, really. Disgusted
with my whole country after the 1984 election, with it bludgeoning
rhetoric of business success, military victory, and contempt for the
failures and oddballs of America who have tried to ask difficult questions, I tried to imagine what it would be like to be in a room with my
own leaders, perhaps inviting the current administration over to my
house for drinks. Aside from their withering scorn that someone so
obviously able and white would choose to live in a shabby house in
an obscure backwater like Minneota (this would provoke only angry
sputtering fulmination from me), I realized that they would bore the
bejesus out of not only me, but everyone I valued and a great many
of those I didn't.

I would rather have spent an evening with Pauline Bardal, playing music and listening to her Icelandic stories. This poor, presumably ignorant and obscure woman would even have taken the fun out of the drinks, since she disapproved of them, yet she was more fit to organize society than the most exalted leaders on the planet. She was not empty as a human, and therefore, however ordinary, gave off love, and could not be boring in quite the same way. Since she had a genuine feeling for beauty, though little skill at making it, "good will" and some richness of soul would enter a room with her and grace it. And yet she was one of millions in a culture that had been bamboozled for reasons no one quite understands into accepting a cheap destructive idea of success and publicly worshiping it in the most demeaning and mindless way. That success idea surfaced like a hydra after every American disaster that ought to have taught us something about ourselves, history, and love—the Viet Nam War, the Depression, the imperialist fiascos with Spain and the Phillipines at the turn of the century, the Civil War. Here is Whitman, the poet of boistrous optimism, as high schools teach him, describing the spiritual life of America in 1870 in his sad essay, *Democratic Vistas:*

> I say we had best look our times and lands searchingly in the face, like
> a physician diagnosing some deep disease. Never was there, perhaps,
> more hollowness at heart than at present, and here in the United States.
> Genuine belief seems to have left us. The underlying principles of
> the States are not honestly believed in (for all this hectic glow, and
> these melodramatic screamings), nor is humanity itself believed in.
> What penetrating eye does not everywhere see through the mask?
> The spectacle is appalling. We live in an atmosphere of hypocrisy
> throughout. The men believe not in the women, nor the women in the
> men. A scornful superciliousness rules in literature. The aim of all

the *Literateurs* is to find something to make fun of. A lot of churches, sects, etc., the most dismal phantasms I know, usurp the name of religion. Conversation is a mass of badinage. From deceit in the spirit, the mother of all false deeds, the offspring is already incalculable. An acute and candid person, in the revenue department in Washington, who is led by the course of his employment to regularly visit the cities of the north, south, and west, to investigate frauds, has talked much with me about his discoveries. The depravity of the business classes of our country is not less than has been supposed, but infinitely greater. The official services of America, national, state, and municipal, in all their branches and departments, except the judiciary, are saturated in corruption, bribery, falsehood, maladministration; and the judiciary is tainted. The great cities reek with respectable as much as non-respectable robbery and scoundrelism. In fashionable life, flippancy, tepid amours, weak infidelism, small aims, or no aims at all, only to kill time. In business (this all-devouring modern word, business), the one sole object is, by any means, pecuniary gain. The magician's serpent in the fable ate up all the other serpents; and moneymaking is our magician's serpent, remaining today sole master of the field. The best class we show, is but a mob of fashionably dressed speculators and vulgarians. True, indeed, behind this fantastic farce, enacted on the visible stage of society, solid things and stupendous labors are to be discovered, existing crudely and going on in the background, to advance and tell themselves in time. Yet the truths are none the less terrible. I say that our New World democracy, however great a success in uplifting the masses out of their sloughs, in materialistic development, products, and in a certain highly deceptive superficial popular intellectuality, is, so far, an almost complete failure in its social aspects, and in really grand religious, moral, literary, and aesthetic results. In vain do we march with unprecedented strides to empire so colossal, out-vying the antique, beyond Alexander's, beyond the proudest sway of Rome. In vain have we annexed Texas, California, Alaska, and reach north for Canada and south for Cuba. It is as if we were somehow being endowed with a vast and more and more thoroughly appointed body, and then left with little or no soul.

It could as well have been written in 1985. This is the failure you get if you begin and proceed with a phony notion of success. This failure, which the culture calls "success," is true spiritual death, not the "death in things," but hell, as Milton conceived it: death in the midst of life, because the world itself, the universe, is dead from inside out, and we carry the corpse with us into every conversation and act.

THE POOR AND THE DRUNK: TWO MORE KINDS OF FAILURE

Two failures we teach children to fear are poverty and alcoholism. We state them positively: work hard and stay sober. Yet Christianity, to which we give public lip service, praises glad poverty; many alcoholics date the birth of their true humanity from the realization of booze's awful power in their lives.

James Agee, in the course of spending a summer writing about some poor ignorant Alabama tenant farmers in the thirties, discovered that their small, failed lives could not quite be described by normal American power values. He calls his book about them *Let Us Now Praise Famous Men* and comes to this conclusion about the poor and failed: they are human in precisely the same manner as ourselves, and therefore bottomless. It takes him hundreds of pages of thundering prose to grab the scruff of the reader's neck, and shake him to the same conclusion. Money earned, suit brand, car model, school degree, powerful army, big bombs, bootstrap rhetoric, make no difference. Everything the success culture takes for granted turns to fog that burns off when you put light on it. At the bottom of everything is skin; under that, blood and bone. This simple fact shocked Agee and gave him a case of the ecstasy.

We feel it even more in the simple, direct photographs Walker Evans took as pendant to Agee's prose. Those, for god's sake, he seems to say, are children, real children, and that is a shoe, and that is a table, even though so badly carpentered of rough wood that it stands on a short leg. What should we tell that child to succeed at, since it is already demonstrably a child? Should we tell it to wash, and put on a good shirt? What should we say to the shoe? Make yourself new, close up your cracked sole, polish yourself, grow into a boot?

Like poverty, alcoholism is a failure hard to deny, for denial leads to suicide. The ideas that Alcoholics Anonymous proposed to help alcoholics recover have in them the "true regret from the heart" that Forster speaks about, and staying sober requires "good will and more good will." An alcoholic must confess to his fellows: all greetings begin, "My name is Joe, and I'm a drunk." Substitute your own name in that sentence and music of failure sounds in earshot. Drunks black out, remember nothing; AA requires memory, the acknowledgment of actions' effects on self and others, then apology and atonement. You must make right what you have put wrong with your drinking; pay just debts. Imagine America coming up from one of its blackouts to apologize to Cambodia, Nicaragua, the Sioux, interned Japanese, or the blacklisted. Imagine yourself. . . .

The serenity prayer, spoken at every AA meeting, is the true national anthem of the country of failure Gilgamesh dreamed about when his conscience tired of brutalizing Uruk, and longed for the true failure in humanity:

God, grant me the serenity to accept the things I cannot change; the courage to change the things I can; and the wisdom to know the difference.

No bombs bursting in air in that one.

FAILURE IN NATIONAL LIFE: A LITTLE HISTORY OF ICELAND

What, then, shall we say in praise of the Bardals, all dead in a hundred years in America, and failed miserably by almost every definition our culture offers us? In my judgment, our false language of power and success, and its consequent notion of sweeping genuine failure harmful to other humans and ourselves under the rug, has left us no true language (except perhaps poetry or song) to describe or think about their lives and thus absorb their history into our own. Without that acknowledgment of failure, memory disappears, history ceases to exist accurately and is of no use to us. We drive by the cemetery a thousand times and cannot see or remember the names written on the stones.

The Bardals came out of an immigrant culture that had succeeded at failure. They were Icelanders, and conscious of it, and though none of Frithgeir's children ever saw their ancestral home, they called themselves "western Icelanders," and could observe by looking at any television set that they were not quite American in the manner conceived in commercials and soap operas.

The Icelandic immigration at the end of the nineteenth century took place, as did so many such movements, largely because of grinding poverty. The Icelanders, historically, showed talent for surviving near-starvation, but, by 1875, an escape opened to them that was like none other in history. Free land was not an offer taken lightly.

At thirty-six I went to live in Iceland for a year or two, and had a look at the farms the ancestors of Minneota Icelanders left, including my own grandfather's and the Bardals'. In 1875, the houses must have been dank turf-covered hovels, smelling of chamber pots and boiled fish, ceilings so low that generally tall Icelanders must have developed hunches stooping under their own roofline. In 1875, there were no roads, only horse tracks; no sophisticated machines, only scythes and hand rakes; almost no light, heat, sanitation, or plumbing. Aside from a handful of Christmas raisins or prunes, and daily rutabagas and potatoes, their whole diet consisted of boiled dried cod, boiled salt mutton, rotted shark, and pudding made out of sour milk. They had never seen an orange, an apple, or corn, much less an avocado. They had little topsoil, a miniscule growing season sufficient for almost no food crops, interminable winters and grey, cold, drizzly summers, frosts in June, snow in August, and icy sea fogs in between. They raised hardy old Viking sheep, a cow or two for milk, and hay that was really only native grass, to feed the animals. They moved around on small sturdy horses who coped with endless frost heaves, bogholes, cliffs, and gravelly, cold, glacial rivers that separated one remote farm from the next. Icelandic farmers lived, for all practical purposes, in the twelfth century until well into the twentieth. It is almost impossible for us to conceive the meanness and isolation of their lives. They occupied the outer edge of an island on the outer edge of Europe in poverty worthy of the most dismal backwater of the third world in Africa or Asia.

Iceland also had a history of losing, both geological and political. Settled by ninth-century Vikings who organized the world's first genuine Parliament, they were the only kingless Europeans but lost that prize through their own interminable squabbling. Birch trees held in their loose but fertile volcanic soil, which they squandered by denuding the countryside for firewood. Even the elements conspired against them. They built up new areas into fertile farmland by painstaking labor after which a neighborhood volcano blew up, burying the field under burning ash. The climate, temperate when they came, soon returned to its true arctic disposition and froze out their hay. Polar ice hugged the shore, as if trying to finish the poor Icelanders off for being impetuous and foolish enough to try to settle this unlikely island and make a civilization out of it.

And yet they did indeed make a great, though curiously austere, civilization. With no usable building stone, no musical instruments, no minable metals, and a paucity of food and shelter, they built the most substantial European literature of the middle ages by using the only equipment left to them on this barren rockpile: language, not Latin, but their own beloved vernacular Icelandic.

What is the heroic subject of the greatest of that literature? Failure. *The Sturlunga Saga* chronicles with bloody detail the venial civil quarrels that led to the breakdown of political structures and ensuing loss of independence. Snorri's *Prose Edda* consisted partly of a versification manual for a kind of poetry, a few hundred years obsolete when Snorri wrote it, that no one would ever write again except as a literary exercise, and partly a history of the old Norse mythology that was by that time utterly obliterated by Christianity and forgotten in the rest of Europe. *Laxdaela Saga* records a willful woman's successive failed marriages and loves that make *Anna Karenina* or *Madame Bovary* seem by comparison cheerful. The gods themselves, in Viking mythology, were doomed to perish, and Valhalla is a temple of failure. In *Njal's Saga* (a worthy companion to Homer) almost all the main characters are swept up in a violent tide that culminates in the deliberate burning to death of Njal's whole family, including aged wife and grandchildren, inside his house. It is surely a cautionary story, designed to be told to an audience themselves afflicted with a quarrelsome nature and taste for recrimination and revenge. The book ends in spent vengeance, and a surfeit of charred, beheaded, stabbed, chopped, impaled corpses that shames the final scenes of *Hamlet* or *Lear*. The human failure in *Njal's Saga* is of such size it attains majesty, but the gods are not blamed for any of it.

The Icelanders, by facing the drastic failures of their history and nature, created a literature that held the national ego together through six hundred years of colonial domination, black plague, leprosy, volcanic eruption, and famine that by 1750 reduced this already half-starved population to half the size it had been at its settlement time. The most wretched Icelandic household had those books and read them; Gunnar, Njal, Gudrun, Egil, and Grettir were the ballast every Icelander carried through the long centuries of failure.

A saga reader visiting Iceland now, expecting blood-thirstiness or violence from the population, is in for disappointment. He finds instead a mild, harmonious, democratic welfare state, just and literate, almost without murder, theft, or any violent crime. Doors are left unlocked and lost billfolds returned to strangers.

Poverty in any sense an American might understand is unknown. It struck me while I lived there, and must equally strike many American tourists, that Iceland *is* what America *says* it is and is, in fact, not. Our literature, too, is full of failure—the sunk Pequod and the dead crew in *Moby Dick*, Hawthorne's vision of failed love in an icy community, Huck Finn on the raft choosing evil, and Whitman's great poems in praise of death—but we do not carry these books around inside our public life as Icelanders carry theirs.

What distinguishes Icelandic from American failure is the sense of responsibility. It was neither Norwegian, Dane, black plague, nor polar ice who wrecked Iceland's independence, fertility and

prosperity; their literature makes absolutely clear that it was Icelanders themselves who did these things. We made terrible mistakes and
we alone, they say to one another in books. Viewing their history generously, you might even be inclined to share blame for troubles with
Norway, Denmark, or at least bad luck, but Icelanders will have none
of it. It is a matter of national pride to have behaved so stupidly in the
past and survived as a nation to learn something from it. Alteration is
possible if you stop in time; this is one of the clear lessons both of AA
and of history. In addition, there is a certain pleasure that comes from
swallowing your own failure. A great deal of Icelandic humor grows
out of these indigestible lumps of history.

Nothing that is *itself* can conceivably be termed a failure by the
transcendental definition. But things must acknowledge and live up to
their selfness. This is fairly effortless for a horse or a cow, more difficult for a human being, and judging by the evidence of history, almost
impossible for a community or a country. When it happens occasionally, as I argue that it did in the case of the Icelanders, it creates a rare
wonder, a community that has eaten its own failures so completely
that it has no need to be other than itself. Iceland has no army, because
an army cannot defend anything genuinely worth defending. In my
more melancholy utopian moments, I think America would be better
defended without one, too.

The Bardals came out of that failure tradition, and it schooled
them well for their hundred years in America. Friends of mine meeting Pauline for the first time would remark on her aristocratic bearing.
There was no bowing and scraping in her; she met bank presidents
and failed farmers with the same straightforward kindness. And why,
given the Declaration of Independence, the Constitution, and the
rhetoric of American history, should she not? Her soul was not tied
to a bank account or elegant clothes, and whatever difficulties life dealt

her, she remained Pauline and that was sufficient. No one can steal the self while you are sleeping if it is sufficiently large in your body. A country with a sufficient ego casts off paranoia about plots to steal its factories and merchandise, and behaves with grace and mildness toward its neighbors.

But an alcoholic protects that weak self by filling it with whiskey. A stock speculator in the twenties filled it with Dusenbergs, ermines, Waterford chandeliers, and Newport villas. When these toys disappeared abruptly, the now defenseless self stepped to the window and, taking advantage of the fact that it lived inside a heavy body, dropped out. Some alcoholics drive off cliffs if you take whiskey away. An empty country, then, protects itself at all costs against the idea of its own failure, lest some part of its weak psyche understand that it must commit a sort of suicide whenever it is tempted to feel the "true regret." A hundred years ago, this was serious, but not final. A country more or less blown off the map, even a large one, would still be populated by deer, muskrats, fox, weeds, and grass. Since 1945, self-building has become a matter of life and death for the whole planet. We have now reached the point in human history where some cure is absolutely necessary, some embracing of wholesome failure.

A REPRISE OF WALT WHITMAN: REAL AND TRANSCENDENTAL FAILURE

I return now to Whitman, who had two ideas about failure, the first transcendental, and the second political. The "natural facts" as Emerson defines them in *Nature*, were not revealing cheerful news about the "spiritual facts" of American life after the Civil War. I argue that the news is no better now, maybe worse, since more time, more evidence, and more material progress have passed our way. Whitman wrote his first joyful hymn to failure in 1855, in the first edition of *Leaves of*

Grass; his attack on "hollowness of heart" came sixteen years later, in 1871. Those years were, prior to our own generation, the most rendingly violent and tempestuous time in American history, but I think we have surpassed them.

Think first of our own conventional notion of failure, and how it differs from either Whitman's. Success involved getting power, money, position, sensual gratification, and the attendant public symbols for these things. Not to acquire them, but to be schooled in a culture that wants you to want them, is our idea of failure.

Think next of "hollowness of heart" as Whitman's language for what we, living in an age of psychology, call the weak ego, or the empty self. How do you fill an ego, make a self strong? The ego requires first the power to sympathetically imagine something outside itself: the lives of other human beings, perhaps enormously different from your own; second, the capacity to love something outside the self in the world of nature, art, or human beings. True symbols of fullness of heart exist only in nature, and cannot be put on credit cards: rocks, weeds, animals, air, water, weather, and other people.

Whitman had experienced profound conventional failure in his own life by the time of his great attack: he saw the horrors of a Civil War hospital as a volunteer nurse for the dying; he lost a government job for writing obscene poetry; he suffered strokes that eventually crippled him; he found no true audience for *Leaves of Grass;* he endured the most corrupt national administration before Nixon's. Yet still he beats and pounds for the failed generals with his transcendental notion of failure. Something succeeds if it is itself: victor and defeated, living and dead, are not separate states but a continuum, success and failure only different faces of the same thing.

Music is a good metaphor for this idea, since it also is a tissue, a continuum, a process. How heavy is music's body? Does it own much land? What sound investments can it make? Does music slice vegetables with a knife or electricity? Does music like sunny climates and lovely cities or is it willing to endure Minneota? Is music bored with the "Largo" from *Xerxes*? Do old ladies' wrong notes offend music's ears? What hymns should you sing at music's funeral? Would music prefer quiche Lorraine or boiled potatoes? What is the gross national product of music? Does music worship Jesus, or the other way around?

When is music ever finally done? Basho (translated by Robert Bly), says

> *The temple bell stops ringing*
> *But the sound keeps coming*
> *Out of the flowers*

Even Minneota flowers . . .

A CODA: THE STILL SMALL VOICE OF MINNEOTA

This has been a long incoherent journey toward this idea. The reader must perhaps exercise "good will" and remember that the whole culture, perhaps the whole weight of western civilization, is against it. The English language even denies it, as one tries to bulldoze a word from one definition to another. And yet, I know it's true. What proof have I offered? The life of Pauline Bardal and her family, a poor tiny country on the edge of the arctic, a half dozen books, experience, some music, finally only a feeling . . . not much. Yet in every artery in my body, and in yours too, that music of failure plays—continually. It sounds like Bach to me, and you must make up your mind what it sounds like to you.

Should you not hear it where you are now, let me remind you that it plays in Minneota, Minnesota, daily, under the water tower, or deep inside the grain elevator bins. You do not need the price of a bus ticket to arrive here, since it is where you are now, wherever that is. You must simply decide to be here, and then you will be.

Always remember, though, that it is a real place in both senses of that word, though not much of a place in American terms. It will never make it on television, though it has ground, water, sky, weather, all the ingredients of placeness. It has pianos, clarinets, and songs too, though it wants violins, and the wind that blows over it comes from Prague and Nairobi and Auckland and brings part of them to live in it. Its humans are often tedious, but sometimes astonishing, here as elsewhere, and the endless weather talk once had a piece of poetry under it. The Bardals lived here, still do in a way, under stones with their names, but in air, too, that comes into the house when you take off the storm windows in spring. I live here now, and plan to always, wherever I am.

Whatever failure is, Minneota is not it. Nothing can be done about living here. Nor should it be. The heart can be filled up anywhere on earth.

COLD SNAP

At thirty below, I try to start the car. A dead groan. No surprise. I go back in the house, call the jump truck, then bundle more to go out and wait. Northwest wind, not one cloud, nothing breathing, bright insane sunlight. I lift up the car hood. Impossible! That should not be there. At the center of the motor lies a gold kitten, torso under heater hose, head nestled against carburetor. Not thinking, I reach in to pet the cat—a fur brick. Must have felt motor heat three days ago, crawled inside to escape that wind and gone to sleep, warm at least for a few minutes. Probably dead in half an hour. It's a vampire, this engine: sleeps by day in an iron coffin, needs heat and blood from something alive to move.

The jump truck comes. As the man clamps the red and white stethoscope wires to the car's chest, he examines the cat: "Poor devil . . . too god-damn cold out here for anything." The car, hit by a lightning bolt from the truck, lurches back to life. Exhaust fog rolls around, trying to cover up that frozen sun. In a few minutes, the carburetor loosens its grip on the cat. It lifts like a family heirloom pried off the corpse finger. The cat is heavy as a field stone in my hand. You could use it as a club, kill something. The motor squirts fog squiggles.

It's not so good here for the harmless and trusting who lay their heads down to sleep with the dead that smooth the pillow for them, pull down the covers, stand beckoning, smiling, efficient. Those dead, all over the earth, want your heat. Now.

I get in the car and drive away to talk to schoolchildren. Later in the day, it makes a try for me too, but I remembered the cat.

SPRING COMES

I

I spend my first spring on the desert among thirty-foot saguaro cactus, thorny arms drooping under rain-bloated weight. Thirsty for so long, drinking everything that comes their way like dry drunks falling off the wagon, they topple over from their own greed. Inside, a spongy skeleton with an old pig's face. Having settled in this unlikely place the saguaro live stubbornly for a long time, die like abruptly slaughtered animals. Past the cactus flows a tan gravel ribbon; the sign says it is a river, warns about lethal floods that last fifteen minutes. Afterward the river turns back into a dust storm and blows around scratching your car. Things here bite and prickle if you touch them: rivers, plants, lizards. The ocotillo, a dehydrated octopus trapped in gravel, waves shiny red fingernail blossoms, as if to say: Shame on you! Go home now.

II

Spring in Minnesota, May snow nothing but black mush. Driving over prairies tonight, the car fills up with wet manure smell. Nothing keeps it out! Every barn in the county shoveled out today; the steering wheel smells of it, radio music too, my mustache saturated, the smell of things going back to work after this long sleep. Daylight comes, and black and pale green earth stretches out to the start of sky. The Yellow Medicine Creek climbed out of its banks, swept up dead brush, swelled into a little Nile foaming briskly along, with its mouth full of winter frost. Under a bare willow, blue violets bloom, hardly an inch high, but blue a mile deep in the petals. Something inside wants its first soak in the creek, to celebrate the beginning of water, the sun's birthday.

A LITTLE TALK FOR THE SCHOOLTEACHERS OF APPLETON, MINNESOTA

We grow up in a practical place where we are encouraged to be reasonable, keep our expectations of the world down, not get too excited. When not engaged in work, or when the world is genuinely mysterious and puzzling (as it so often is), when love or grief rear up in our life—in other words, when feeling is demanded from us—we feel embarrassed, inadequate, uncomfortable. Think how difficult it is for people to say honest, consolatory things after funerals, embrace others' bodies during weddings, or express pleasure at the beautiful, whether ice crusts on dry weeds, a bumper crop of beans, or the expression on a stranger's face. Retirement is hard on us, and deprived of practical physical life we lose our minds and die too soon. I had an aunt who forgot who she was the moment she had no one left to feed.

Schools do not help us in these things as they ought to, nor, for that matter, do churches. They, too, are products of hard weather and north European stolidness. We seldom counsel high school students that it is all right to live an unconventional life. We think bookish, overly sensitive students so poorly adjusted to life in Appleton or Minneota that everyone hopes that they go off to the cities where they will be happier and "fit" better. Yet we ought to encourage precisely these students to remain in small towns or on farms. They can help the rest of us in our feeling lives, our marriages, the stretch of years when it no longer is of much importance to win the big game or prepare for a mechanical job in agribusiness.

In my experience, people in western Minnesota have to get drunk before they dance. They take pleasure in the body working but not moving joyfully and skillfully to music of whatever kind. Dance is connected with feeling life, and schools and churches ought to help us dance better, whatever the beauty or grace in our individual bodies. By dance I mean, of course, whatever is not practical for beans on the north eighty, and therefore connects our inner life with other human beings.

Bill Valgardson is a writer of Icelandic descent from Gimli, Manitoba, a farming and fishing town north of Winnipeg, bleaker, more full of mosquitoes than even Appleton or Minneota. I met him recently in Victoria, B.C., where he now teaches. I asked him how a practical prairie boy adapted to the Canadian version of San Diego. At first he disliked it, he said, because the weather was too good, people too lazy. Work wasn't done passionately as in Gimli. But he soon weakened and began to leave his office early, took up rock climbing and folk dancing with a local amateur troupe. Now in his mid-forties, he says, "It's hard for me to get my work done and dance as much as I want to. Maybe I'll retire early." Then he made an extremely interesting distinction: "People in Gimli have a job—and that's what they talk about. Here they have an income and you frequently don't know or care where it comes from. The important thing is how you use your earned money to do what pleases you most, and explore the world."

It's a little far-fetched to imagine that Appleton or Minneota will take up that habit of mind soon, but there's something that the school system can learn from it. Instead of just training students for the practical life of work, we ought to think more about training them (and ourselves too) to use that income gotten from work often not pleasant or interesting, to feed our own feeling part, or to put it in somewhat different terms, irrigate the soul, so it can grow something that might illuminate the difficult parts in our own lives. We do this with arts, not job training—and while its cost-effectiveness may not appeal to the average western Minnesota taxpayer, its psychological benefits for a whole community life are incalculable.

I close with a poem of mine which I wrote for my students at Southwest State University. It begins with Carl Jung's idea that the wild, passionate, sometimes uncivilized inner life of human beings is best symbolized by your sexual opposite. The inner life of a woman is a young boy; that of a pale Scandinavian like me is a black-haired girl. Either we make friends with this opposite, though it makes us no money, or it turns vicious and poisons our conscious lives. This is not practical; it is necessary. The poem started as advice for my students, but is also advice for you, for stolid Minnesotans, northern Protestants, and most of all, me. Here's the poem:

Advice

Someone dancing inside us
learned only a few steps:
the "Do-Your-Work" in $^4/_4$ *time,*
the "What-Do-You-Expect" waltz.
He hasn't noticed yet the woman
standing away from the lamp,
the one with black eyes
who knows the rumba,
and strange steps in jumpy rhythms
from the mountains in Bulgaria.
If they dance together,
something unexpected will happen.
If they don't, the next world
will be a lot like this one.

LUCKY STONE

The Minneota Chevy dealer sells forty-two Chevies, and he and his wife win a trip to Athens and the islands, all expenses paid by General Motors, so they're right there on the Acropolis and the guide talks about Socrates, old gods, marble statues of Athena that stood in the Parthenon, Turkish shells lobbed onto the roof in the eighteenth century, missing marbles stolen by the British Museum, and a lot more too. Then they all go have an ouzo and rest up for dinner. It's amazing where Chevies get you in America!

Later, back in Minneota, where blizzards howl, corn grows, and the world's oldest exposed rock is close by in Granite Falls where the last glacier gouged out the Minnesota River Valley floor, a small chunk of marble cornice sits on the purchase order pile in the back room of the Chevy garage. "A hunk of the Parthenon," LeRoy says to customers. "Got her on my trip."

Later yet, drunk in the liquor store, LeRoy says to the bartender, "Tom, I got a present for you." He hands him the discolored marble chunk. Tom takes it home and keeps it until he hears that Bill Holm is going off to Greece to sleep with the noise of the Aegean in his ears. He goes to Bill's with the rock and says, "Here, take this with you. I think it's lonesome, so take it home."

It's the length of my index finger, nestles easily in its thumb cradle. The top is white as the Parthenon in old paintings, robed men circling its columns, deep in history's best arguments. But the edges, once pure

white, are discolored by years of dirt and gunpowder, turned now the
used shade of real skin. Still you almost feel Plato's hands when you
touch it. This is a lucky stone: it will go home now. If a stone sang, it
would be singing:

I'm a lucky stone;
I've traveled now,
seen corn and beans,
felt mad winter,
heard new speech,
wind in fall grass.
Chevies mortgaged under me
roared over gravel roads
to farms owned also
by the bank. Belgians
and Icelanders handled me,
wondered if this
was Catholic or
Lutheran stone.
But time to go home;
I need that history
no one wanted though
it was their own,
need heat and sea,
moon on white hills;
so I go to Athens now,
sing: lucky stone
lucky stone, lucky stone.

AT THE GRAVE OF WILLIAM J. HOLM: BAY VIEW CEMETERY, BELLINGHAM, WASHINGTON

Grandfather Sveinn made it halfway across the continent to the prairies in Minneota, Minnesota, and Great-Grandfather Johannes continued the rest of the way to die at Bellingham Bay, Pacific in front of him, volcano behind him, two more sons laid out under the same tree. Born in north Iceland, he came halfway around the globe to find the same saltwater and lava he left behind.

When I first came to see the graves, I went to the Icelandic old folks' home in Blaine, on the Canada border, and announced that I was William Holm. One ancient Icelander glared at me and said, *"Thu ert ekki Villi Holm; thu ert bara unglingar; hann do fjorartiu og fimm."* (You are not Willy Holm; you are only a youngster. He died in '45.)

"No," I say. "He was my father's uncle, all three of us with the same name. What was he like?" I ask.

"He was a farmer, a big, even-tempered, quiet man who loved to sing!"

"Any Holms left around here?"

"No. All dead. No children."

On my fortieth birthday, I stand here next to my own name on this gravestone: William J. Holm, born Korekstathir 1860, came to Minnesota about 1880, to Washington with the new century, buried in

Bellingham the year that Hiroshima and Dresden happened. Descriptions of those unnatural fires must have seemed to Villi like Askja erupting when he was fifteen. Sheep and hay died then, Japanese and Germans now. It takes a volcano to make an American, or to unmake one.

Here, Villi, is your grandnephew looking down toward you, hoping for whatever wisdom can be found in the meager facts about your lonesome life, willing to offer you whatever love and honor one owes blood and the gift of a name. I sing too, am big, probably more nervous and noisy than you, but I found the Pacific all right, and bring along what cellular energy is left of your brother. No more fire erupted lately, either from your new volcano, Baker, or from the airplanes of your new country.

America ends twenty miles north of here, and two miles west. We are both painted into a tight corner, waiting to see if things will dry soon enough for us to get out without leaving footprints.

IS MINNESOTA IN AMERICA YET?

A few years ago, after working myself into a state of high moral dudgeon over one of America's several recent wars, or government-sponsored financial scandals, or servings of one too many dollops of sanctimonious hypocrisy in public speech, I proposed secession to my neighbors in Minneota, even suggesting that our local senator start the legal process of severance in the legislature. Technically, this is treason, I suppose, but Minneotans (like all their fellow Minnesotans) take news of major crimes and catastrophes calmly. It is the small ones— joining the county library, the new wastewater plant, the mileage on the second police car—that push them over into indignation.

"I've had it with Washington," I said righteously. "They take a half-billion cash for defense out of the Second Congressional District and give us Grenada (or Libya, or Panama, etc.). We could defend ourselves for a fraction of that, put a few of the boys from the liquor store on the South Dakota and Iowa borders with a little beer and a case or two of shotgun shells. They'd keep the Grenada militia or Noriega's storm troops safely outside Minneota. Then we could take the half-billion and pay off the farm debt. "In fact," I continued from behind my invisible podium, "if we don't declare outright independence and seal the borders at Luverne and Hendricks, we can always join the Canadians. They're having trouble with Quebec, anyway, and could use another province in the south. We'd have civilized health insurance at last, better fishing, and a musically and morally superior anthem." ("O Canada" is, by any standard, an improvement on "The Star-Spangled Banner." It is gentle and singable, with lyrics more full of praise and sweetness than blood and guts.)

After a few long sighs, a roll of the dice for coffee, and a pull or two on a hat brim, I got responses like: "Well, they got that good wheat pool up there; I believe a fellow could do a little better on grain prices then." Or "the beer up there sure is stronger—the Canadians don't go for that 'lite' stuff." Or "my wife's cousin farms up by Brandon. He was laid up with a hernia operation last year—says it didn't cost a thing, and the hospital was real nice." And more . . . In the middle of the chest-thumping patriotic gunboat eighties, I seemed to have uncovered a live strain of secessionist sentiment, plain citizens ready to move the border south, or to declare independence, like a Balkan republic or South Carolina, and get on with the business of daily life, minus Washington. "From sea to shining sea" had shrunk from Big Stone Lake on the Dakota border all the way to Lake Superior.

Are these plain farmers and neighbors poor Americans, or has the process not quite gotten finished inside them? It's one thing to be an external American—just in ceremony, like Charlemagne baptizing the German army by marching it through the Rhine—but what does it mean, in an interior sense, to be American? Has Minnesota joined the union yet, psychologically? The possible answers to these questions may be more interesting and less obvious than we imagine.

Begin with the commonplace notion of Minnesota smugness— the feeling we have that we are somehow cleaner, more virtuous, harder working, better governed, more boring but more civilized than "them," whoever "they" are. Any reader of the essay can think quickly of ten examples of it: in newspapers, political speeches, church sermons, coffee-table talk. Turn on public radio, and you will hear the tune, sometimes a shy countermelody, sometimes tutti fortissimo . . .

It is not our most attractive quality as a state. But is it true?

Partly. Daniel Elazar, in *Cities of the Prairie*, describes Minnesota up to the sixties with uncanny accuracy. He first remarks on the nastiness of Minnesota's climate and terrain we all know and love so well. This "difficult physical environment," Elazar writes, "led to the establishment of marginal civilization, one which was prone to seek more radical solutions to its recurrent problems." Its politics, he continues, were "dominated by issues, mostly highly moral in character." This moralism was "reinforced by a majority of Minnesota's first settlers, who stemmed from a moralistic political culture," and who, "unlike the Yankee settlers of Illinois, were virtually the first to occupy" Minnesota, and therefore "did not have to compromise their communitarian notions with any 'rugged' individualistic elements already entrenched in power."

The second wave of immigrants, huger and ultimately dominant, came directly from Scandinavia, Germany, and Ireland "to Minnesota, where they settled on virgin land. Thus, unlike their compatriots who settled in cities or rural areas already occupied by others and who had to adjust their ways to established patterns, they could retain many of the basic attitudes . . . they had brought with them from the Old World. . . . They created replicas of Old World farm villages, each with its own distinctive culture." I thought of a fifty-mile radius of Minneota: the Tyler Danes, the St. Leo Germans, the Wilno Poles, the Milan Norwegians, the Ghent Belgians, the Edgerton Dutch, the Clarkfield Swedes, the Clontarf Irish, the Minneota Icelanders. "They brought with them a kind of proletarian radicalism to add to an already radical (by American standards) tradition of politics in Minnesota." Think of the Farmer-Labor Party, the Nonpartisan League, the McCarthy campaign of 1968, the high taxes and good social services, the disquieting un-Americanism of voting in the last twenty-five years of presidential elections. Minnesotans tackle political problems "in a spirit of communalism and political responsibility akin to that found among their fathers." Finally, "unlike . . . Illinois, politics in Minnesota consistently has been an activity open to and dominated by amateurs. This may be due to the persistence of issues as a central element in determining alignments." Well, of course, we say with some pride. "What *other* than issues? Who *else* than amateurs?" Elazar's book doesn't throw much of a monkey wrench into Minnesota smugness.

An old friend once had pencils printed to give away as Christmas presents. They said, "Hooray for Minnesota! We never voted for Reagan or Bush or anyone like them!" True enough. We lived up to our reputation for cranky isolation from the political fashions of the eighties, until the map of non-Reagan America showed *only* Minnesota and Washington, D.C.

I remember as a boy in the fifties having a high regard for almost all the politicians in Minnesota, even those I disagreed with, and (probably under heavy influence of listening to my father curse them for crookedness, ignorance, and venality) disliking every national figure—with special contempt for Nixon and Ezra Taft Benson. But men like Humphrey, McCarthy, Stassen, Floyd Olson, Elmer Benson, Elmer Andersen, and Walter Judd—the fierce anticommunist China-lobby man—could be trusted to speak fine direct English in complete sentences (with clauses!), to have their hands in no one's pockets, to keep their discourse to ideas and policies and away from cheap innuendo. They seemed honest, decent men of high intelligence, *public servants* in the old sense of both those words. Whether this was true or not made no difference, so long as an entire community *perceived* it to be true. It was the cement inside people's sense of themselves as citizens. "We" were not like "them," represented by fools and crooks.

In the election of 1954, the Republicans ran Valdimar Bjornson, the state treasurer and a Minneota Icelander of immense local fame and repute, against Hubert Humphrey, in those days so impregnable that if Christ himself had returned in glory to run for the Senate, the old farmers might have said, "Well, Jesus is a wonderful fellow, but I believe Hubert would still be the better senator." Although I was ten years away from voting, it created a great conflict for me. I had met Hubert at a Farmers Union meeting at the Swede Prairie Township Hall, had shaken his hand, and gotten his autograph in my little red book (I still have it!), and had seen him moving—smiling, affable, and confident—through the crowd of farmers, remembering every name, climaxing the night with a fine tub-thumping speech ending with a unison chorus of "Parity, parity, parity!" At eleven, I thought him a great man.

But I thought Valdimar Bjornson a great man, too, having heard my parents praise him as a model of eloquence and intelligence, a world-class orator who had corralled at least two languages, Icelandic and English, and made them do his bidding at will. And he was an Icelander to boot, sure proof of his greatness! I had even been photographed by the *Minneapolis Star* getting his autograph, a fat, pink, bespectacled boy standing rapt in the presence of greatness signing its name.

How lucky to be a Minnesotan, I remember thinking, and to have no choice but to be represented in the Senate by such human beings. It was an election that couldn't be lost by any citizen. I have often thought of that election since with considerable nostalgia.

This flowering of political decency did indeed arise from some peculiarities of Minnesota as a place—heterogeneous, not long out of the Old Country, and mistrustful of professional politicians. Hubert was raised in a Huron drugstore, Valdimar in the back room of the Minneota newspaper, and if they lost an election, or wearied of public life, they could return happily and ably to filling prescriptions, teaching school, or writing for a newspaper. Their life was not their office, or so we thought, and so we trusted them. No one, on the other hand, could imagine Nixon or Lyndon Johnson with a real job. They were political fish who would dry up out of the water of public life. Jefferson, had he lived long enough to know about Minnesota (the place he bought), would have liked it—yeoman citizens doing their public duty with disinterested intelligence, then returning to plain life without aristocratic pretense or private stashes of public money.

Only now in this last quarter of the century have the fires under the melting pot started to homogenize (or Americanize, if you like) the majority of the Minnesota population. When I was a boy in Minneota, the kindling barely warmed the edges.

I went to a country school eight miles north of Minneota. The teacher, Cora Monseth, was a first-generation Norwegian, and spoke only Norwegian to her aged parents. Of the children, the Orsens, Myhres, Thostensons, and Kompeliens heard Norwegian, the Andersons and the Lindstroms heard Swedish, the Sturms heard German, the Van Moorlehems and Van Hyftes heard Flemish, and I heard Icelandic. Not a single child in that school had a grandfather who spoke English either well or without a heavy brogue, and every parent learned English as a second language. In the fifties, we were the first generation to have *only* English. I was twenty before I met anyone whose grandparents had been in America during the Civil War. For the citizens of Swede Prairie, the Thirty Years' War between the Protestants and the Catholics had more historic relevance than the War between the States. None of our grandparents had even *seen* a Negro slave, much less owned or liberated one.

Immigration was neither so easily accomplished nor so easily finished a psychological process as we like to imagine in our more sentimental moments: on Svenskarnas Dag, Syttende Mai, Christmas Eve. We leave out the grief, the phantom pain from an amputated culture and language, the economic catastrophe, the fear and dread of poverty, the truncated souls who went under. Ole Rölvaag, in his little novel in the form of American letters, *The Third Life of Per Smevik*, has the narrator describe, not instant Americanization, but a sequence in which the first generation gives up its soul, becomes neither American nor Norwegian, but endures a kind of psychic limbo between two worlds. The children make their way only halfway into the new culture, and the third generation finally sloughs off the old like a snakeskin, losing its power along with its misery and becoming, in return, something their own grandfathers wouldn't recognize.

I think Rölvaag is mostly right, but coming a generation or two after him, I've observed the process differently than he could have imagined. The Minnesota immigrant culture became a thing in itself, neither Europe nor America, though with a few toes in both, and a few surprises that neither Europe nor America would have predicted. This third culture had its own beginning, middle, and end, and its own Götterdämmerung built into its origins and structure, probably within a single century. I call it the "pickled in amber" culture, and my generation is the last gasp of the first wave of it in Minnesota. After me, the deluge—the real America.

Minneota, like hundreds of other towns in Minnesota, celebrated its centennial in 1981. I'll use it as an example here, not because it's exceptional in any way, but because it's typical, a regular sort of place in Minnesota terms. It was settled first by a few stray postwar Yankees, some post–potato famine Irish, and Norwegians. The Icelanders arrived soon after, and finally the Flemish-speaking Belgians, and Dutch. At the end of *one* generation, by the turn of the century, the immigration was an accomplished fact. Only stringers and strays arrived later. Starting as a chunk of empty treeless prairie at the end of the Civil War, Minneota arrived at around the current population (1,400) within about twenty years, lightning speed in human history. It boasted a two-story dry goods store, the Dayton's of the prairies and the largest west of Mankato, a brick Gothic Revival school, three or four handsome churches (Lutheran and Catholic, of course), a handful of grand mansions for the newly moneyed, including a Summit Avenue–style beauty crowned with an octagonal tower room and reputedly designed by Cass Gilbert, architect of the Capitol in St. Paul. It had banks, livery stables, hotels, a drugstore, two doctors, and a fine newspaper, the *Minneota Mascot,* that was already on its way to being one of the most influential and highly regarded small-town papers in the Midwest. The town merchants spoke English well (in addition to whatever else), and first-generation immigrant children had already graduated from Minneota High School and gone off to colleges like Gustavus Adolphus and the University of Minnesota, to begin careers as journalists, lawyers, teachers, doctors.

A Minneotan born in Iceland, B. B. Gislason, had gone off to defend America in the Spanish-American War, risking his young Icelandic hide to help acquire Cuba and the Philippines. The town survived a grasshopper plague, a drought, killer blizzards, a bank panic (1893), and a major recession. To all outward appearances, it looked a thoroughly American place, an immigrant success story, a model demonstration of tamed wilderness, quick prosperity, domestic respectability—a triumph for civilization, a proud realization of the promise of America, already beginning to melt its happy well-fixed immigrants down into the democratic soup. And yet . . . and yet . . .

In the 1990s, over a century after settlement, Minneota remains at its turn-of-the-century size, and in this shows amazing luck for a small Minnesota immigrant town. Most have collapsed, lost population, business, and reason for existence, and are on the fast downslide to ghost-town status. Minneota will get there, too, but it will take longer. A handful of old people still speak Scandinavian languages badly, and a handful of middle-aged Belgians keep up Flemish. Business life is mostly out of town. Young people watch a lot of television and can't pronounce their ancestors' names—if they remember them. The Big Store is a furniture storeroom, and the Cass Gilbert house now a duplex, minus its grand curving staircase. The boulevard elms, planted shortly after the turn of the century, arched eighty feet high like a green cathedral over the town until a few short years ago, when they succumbed to the Dutch elm beetle, leaving the town naked on its sun-baked prairie for the second time this century.

Yet the pickled-in-amber culture in Minneota, and in every one of the country towns like it, had an amazing half-life of economic and intellectual energy as it peaked fast and then declined. Take the Icelanders as an example. They arrived around 1880, the poorest and more isolated of Europeans, their physical and mental lives still medieval. Within twenty years they had learned English without losing Icelandic, sent children, even from the poorest families, to college to become lawyers, journalists, and teachers, and had begun a publishing house and a newspaper. They took citizenship, inventing, for the first time in their history, legal family names, but raised bilingual children who, when asked, called themselves not Americans but *Vestur Islend-ingur*—"Western Icelanders." Few immigrants (Icelanders included) wrote many letters home; the long sea voyage was a razor cut between two worlds. Relatives left behind were as good as dead. There was no direct dialing to the old life, no fax number, no e-mail.

Yet for the great issues and events of American history, they were a little out of sync. The Civil War meant nothing, the Depression arrived ten years early with the collapse of land prices, World War II meant high farm prices, civil rights meant going to your children's weddings even if they married Catholics or Lutherans, the communist menace had about as much reality as it really had. Decades arrived five years late; the soporific fifties ended in about 1965, and the counterculture lasted until five years after California freaks had shaved and joined brokerage firms.

Was Minneota really America, and were the backcountry Icelanders, Norwegians, and Belgians really American yet? Of course. They were out of social sync, geographically peripheral, politically grumpy but able to ignore politics, and economically colonized—though comfortable because of the vast surplus of riches of the country. America *is*, or was, a country of peripheries, not of centers. Minnesota is merely a clearer (because *more* out of sync) example of it. There was no large body of people in any small place who had any experience of *being* American, aside from having old citizenship certificates folded among the family heirlooms. The first generation thought, worshipped, and most often married in its own language, but it couldn't go back, and it couldn't run for president. The second generation grew up in a foreign language, cast it off either from distaste, disuse, or marriage outside the circle. By the thirties and forties even Catholic masses and Lutheran services collapsed into English. I am at the tail end of the third generation, born in World War II, who grew up among the ghosts of immigration, in which nationally idiomatic English was a matter of age, not education. Cedric Adams still announced the Minnesota truth on the radio to rural people with brogues and cousins up in the Twin Cities, but television and the economic and social collapse of village life were about to suck us into the orbit of the coasts, of Washington, of the plugged-in rock-and-roll culture. The amber around us had dried and crumbled, and now we could say "Have a good day!" with the best of them.

Here's an example of crumbled amber, of immigrant meltdown, and the way it worked in Minneota. During my high school days at the end of the fifties, the only sexual advice in most houses in Minneota would have astonished a modern teenager. In Scandinavian Lutheran houses, it went like this: "You stay away from the Belgians. Get in trouble with one of them, and they'll take you to the priest and make you turn. You'll have to sign your own children away to Rome. You marry one and I won't darken the church door." Presumably Belgian children listened to some similar version with warnings about lascivious Lutherans who believed in divorce, childless houses, bad food, and watery theology. *Those* churches were not about to get darkened either. Since this advice floated around in the cultural ether, I remember asking my mother about its exact provisions. "Could I marry a Jew, or a Greek, or a black woman, or a Chinese?" If you can find one, she implied, go ahead. They practice birth control, read heterodox books, and don't make you sign children away into the Vatican sinkhole.

Minneotans solved the problem of intolerance promptly and in a very American way. They proceeded briskly to marry the other, while the ethnic church and family identity collapsed in on itself except as a means of passing time in nostalgic conversation. The town now had a good supply of Lutherans with Belgian names, and Catholic Petersons. The first step in becoming a real American is to accumulate strange cousins. The second, less happy step is to forget that you are connected or related to anybody. Minneota hasn't quite arrived there—yet.

But aside from its sexual and religious warnings, the pickled-in-amber culture, while it lasted, had amazing intellectual vitality too. Think of the writers who came out of it: Ole Rölvaag, Herbert Krause, Meridel Le Sueur, and Tom McGrath (compare their political energy with that of a "real" American like Robert Lowell); Fred Manfred, whose finest work is deeply colored with both the language and culture of Friesland; and Robert Bly, whose energy comes partly from his role as an old immigrant Norwegian literary circuit rider, filled with passionate Ibsenesque improving. The ghosts of that immigrant energy are faded but still alive in my own generation. It's not a bad record either politically or culturally for a harsh, out-of-the-way place with a small population. We have done all right by not quite homogenizing.

Sometimes, after elections or televised celebrity trials, or our periodic national eruptions of "America firsters" immigrant hatred, I ask myself, What in me is not homogenized, not melted down, still pickled in amber? The Icelander immigrants gave me two psychic gifts that still operate, one useful to me and the other mostly disastrous—though honorable in a quirky way. The old Icelanders filed and categorized their fellow humans by language skills. An admirable human spoke admirable speech—precise, witty, without jargon or cliché, with nice distinction in diction and vocabulary. The old idea of a "word hoard" survived in them; the better stocked the hoard, the more armed the human. This led to a certain snottiness in daily life. Inarticulate mumbling or highfalutin cant opened for Icelanders the opportunity for lunges of sharp satire and withering disdain. They didn't do well with TV, advertising, or the usual language of national public discourse. That fierce love of language had something to do with my becoming a writer.

The second, less useful gift is the disdain for money—particularly any talk about it. An unrepaid loan gave birth not to arguments but to ice-cold, ax-sharp shunning. You simply didn't speak to people who were guilty of some possibly imaginary shabby behavior about money. To pay serious verbal attention to money diminished you as a human. You can't get rich in America with that kind of attitude, but most of the time, I'm half-grateful to have inherited it.

So what happens now? Has the old pickled-in-amber northern European culture Americanized at last? Minnesota (and by analogy, the United States) seems to me in no danger, as long as new immigrants come in to stir the pot, or to recharge the circuits of economic and intellectual energy. I'll give two examples.

I'm a schoolteacher who complains a lot about the lack of energetic curiosity in students. So many seem bored and listless with the prospect of their own lives, wanting material comfort and security more than high adventure and joyful risk. A few years ago, the college on the southwest prairies where I teach recruited a bunch of Hmong students mostly from the Twin Cities. I taught some of them Freshman English. Their language skills were terrible in one way— mistakes with articles, verb tenses, pronouns, word order; the spelling can only be described as remarkable. Yet their essays were lively and interesting. It was quite clear even through the fog of language mistakes that they had something to say, a story to tell or a point to make, and they wished me (or any reader) to understand it. Their papers had real interior energy despite exterior mistakes. They regarded written language as an instrument of human communication. If you think the previous sentence unnecessary, a self-evident cliché, or blathery edspeak jargon, ask your local teacher, who reads student essays by the pound. From native speakers these days, teachers get mostly pages of words without much accurate observation, without the *world* in them. "You know . . ." has become an instrument of not-knowing, not-seeing, as if the technologized and shrunken planet had passed by a human brain without making much impression.

Not so with the Hmong students. I had essays about tigers on the path to the farm fields, ghosts of murdered Hmong haunting the

Thai resettlement camps in the form of flickering red lights, complaints about arranged marriages, wonderful descriptions of snow from people who first saw it as teenagers. I corrected as much of the grammatical mess as I thought possible and returned the papers. The next day, the papers came back—corrected—with requests for further corrections. And these are students from sometimes illiterate families, learning to write a language their own parents cannot speak, after only six or seven years as immigrants in Minnesota. While those Hmong students will never be "real" Americans psychologically, they will bring that energy, ambition, and curiosity to Minnesota life for a few more generations, before their grandchildren, too, are plugged into the central circuits. In the meantime, I expect a good deal of Minnesota literature to be populated by hungry tigers for the first time in its brief history. That will perk things up for a while.

A few years ago, I got a phone call from a complete stranger who had read my essay called "The Music of Failure," in which I express a kind of discomfort with American notions of success and achievement, and praise the old immigrant culture that I've praised here. The stranger was so taken with my discomfort that he drove to Minneota to meet me. He turned out to be a north Indian physicist who had lived and worked in Minnesota for a long time, was separated from his native Hindu culture by distance, education, and his habit of mind as a scientist and a rationalist. At the same time, he was bored and uneasy with typical Twin Cities talk of duck hunting, bottom-line deals, and "How about those Twins?" Minneota, as I described it, sounded more like his north Indian hometown than other American places.

We became friends and have had long conversations over the years about what it feels like to be an immigrant, to be a Minnesotan, or to be an American. I've learned a lot from him about what the inner lives of my own grandparents must have been like. He has mastered the language, culture, and technology of the modern West as my grandparents never did, but the mastery has not killed off the ghosts of four thousand years of genetic and cultural history. You don't shuck off religions, languages, or cultures easily—they're part of your cellular life.

His aunt visited him recently and I went to meet her and eat some north Indian home cooking. The conversation was translated for my benefit. She upbraided her nephew humorously for not being married yet. It was time for the family to arrange a proper match. I thought of my uncle, Adalbjorn, who was the first of his family to marry a non-Icelander (he married a Norwegian), and my grandfather Herman's angry question, "Couldn't you find an Icelander to marry?" She did a little schoolwork on the *Bhagavad-Gita* (she is a teacher of high school Sanskrit), and then prayed and chanted before dinner for half an hour. "Is it an old prayer?" I asked the physicist. He had never learned the prayer; it was not part of his doctoral work in physics, so he asked his aunt. "No, not old," she said, and then told the story of the origin of the song to Krishna she had just sung. Only from about A.D. 700. Not old. I thought of my delight at finding a gravestone from the 1870s in a Lincoln County graveyard.

Then we sat down to a north Indian feast—course after course of piquant spices, flat bread, interesting vegetables, sticky rice, and no meat. I loved it! Here I am, I thought, smacking my temporarily vegetarian lips, in the land of the steak house, eating delicacies prepared by a citizen of the country in which, not very long ago, it was a capital offense to kill a cow. When I asked my physicist friend what he did for teenage rebellion in a Hindu family, he said he went to the Muslim neighborhoods to eat meat, chewing cardamom seeds on the way home to hide his sins.

He has now taken up landscape painting as a relief from industrial physics and invitations to hockey games and walleye fishing. He rediscovered the treeless prairies and paints them passionately, but with the peculiar eye of someone who grew up looking at the Himalayas and terraced farms just to the north of his hometown. His prairies will look as different from mine as my grandfather's would have—with their ghost images of black volcanic crags, and a cold gray roiling sea. The prairies become a richer place by being observed by people with one eye pointed at each world. So does Minnesota. So, for that matter, does the United States, if indeed we've joined it yet. The un-American (or half-American) sensibility of that pickled-in-amber culture is the dynamo that powers an astonishing number of good things we've done as a country so far.

AFTERWORD: A LEFT BANK CAN BE FOUND ANYWHERE ON EARTH

David Pichaske

When I met Bill Holm in the fall of 1981, he was a project waiting to happen. A decade after leaving the Midwest to pursue adventures in the Fabled East, Bill was back in his hometown of Minneota, Minnesota, by conventional definitions a failure: divorced, childless, without a full-time job, an ambitious writer approaching forty with not one book with his name on the spine. "How strange to think of giving up all ambition," muses Robert Bly, who would become Bill's friend and mentor, a poet who had followed a similar path out of and back to small-town Minnesota. Surely Minneota was no place for an artist! The essays of *The Music of Failure* describe small-potatoes life in a small-potatoes town, a life that must seem supremely inconsequential to American entrepreneurs.

But giving up ambition, Bly points out in the poem I just quoted, allows us to see clearly—and the heart, as Bill comes to realize, can be filled up anywhere on earth. Moreover, nonambition was exactly what interested Americans during the Reagan eighties: a low-key, sane, rural antidote to the over-the-top, urban, frenetic seventies. Robert Bly and William Stafford were joining John Ashbery and Robert Lowell in American literature textbooks, and Garrison Keillor's *A Prairie Home Companion* was laying the groundwork for his

1985 best seller *Lake Wobegon Days*. In his home place, Bill recovered a functioning community of farmers and townspeople—both the material and the audience for the place-based realism that was replacing the dislocated and dislocating postmodernism of the fifties and sixties. At Southwest Minnesota State University in Marshall, Bill found work as an adjunct and then as a full-time professor—and the buzzing literary community resurrected in the anthology he assembled in 2007 for the college's fortieth anniversary, *Farming Words: The Harvest of Literature at a Prairie College*. Among the old ones, Meridel Le Sueur, Fred Manfred, Thomas McGrath, Robert and Carol Bly. Teaching at the college in the early eighties, Phil Dacey, Leo Dangel, Alec Bond, Joe Amato, Don Olsen, and Howard Mohr. Drifting in and out for readings and short assignments, Faith Sullivan, Dave Etter, Norbert Blei, Jim Heynen, Phebe Hanson, Freya Manfred, Linda Hasselstrom, David Allen Evans, Bill Kloefkorn, Mark Vinz, Joe and Nancy Paddock, John Calvin Rezmerski, and Paul Gruchow. Not bad company! Southwest State in the 1980s was kind of an American Left Bank in rural Minnesota, vibrant and quirky. Bill thought he returned home a failure; I thought I had come as an exile. In fact, we had both been lucky as hell, perfectly in step with the times.

The community of students and writers gathered in workshops and evening classes and readings, and on Friday afternoon at the Silver Dollar Bar, in Ghent, Minnesota, between Minneota and Marshall. (These were the days before harassment regulations prohibited or discouraged student–teacher interaction.) Sometimes we talked shop—I remember outlining an entire new literature program in less than two hours in September 1982—but mostly the Silver Dollar Bar was poetry, stories, beer, and California burgers with fries. The college crowd mixed with locals, who were a lot shrewder than stereotypes would have them; college profs preached to, and learned from, the locals. Occasionally (say, every other month) there would be a Cornstock "gathering" at the Ghent Legion Hall. Cornstock was a one-night prairie Woodstock Music and Arts Fair, so named by children of the sixties nostalgic about that great moment in 1969. It was an evening of song, poetry, food, other things, and who knows what adventures. It began with a potluck dinner at 5:30; readings and music started around 7:00. Participants were asked to bring a dish to share and three dollars to cover the costs of the hall rental and a keg of beer. Cornstock in those days was like Harlem before it became commercial, or the Monday night hootenannies during the early days of the Greenwich Village folk music revival. And it cost the state not a penny of tax or grant money.

Gradually Cornstock evolved into Marshall Festival, a weeklong sensory overload of poetry, prose, and fiction invented by Phil Dacey in 1986. Welcome the likes of William Stafford, Wendell Berry, Ted Kooser, Gerald Vizenor, Robert Bly, Eugene McCarthy, plus dozens of writers and musicians and literally hundreds of literary wannabes and fans. Among these celebrities, the locals more than held their own. Reviewing Marshall Fest in *Coda*, Ted Kooser wrote, with one eye toward the Bly farm in Madison and the other on the festival in Marshall, "There are certain spots on the globe where magical lines intersect and wonderful things occur. . . . I have never seen a group of people so happy to see one another." Kooser specifically pointed out Bill Holm as "one of Minnesota's few national treasures."

Although Bill had found part-time adjunct work with the Continuing Education program at Southwest State the year before I came to Minnesota, he and I were hired full time in the fall of 1981—our thirty-eighth years. We both had one-year contracts, after experience elsewhere as teachers, writers, and, in my case, as a publisher. Our experience was valuable to the school; the precariousness of our positions (not even tenure track, let alone tenured) was both a distraction and a motivation to us. We worked our butts off. We covered for each other in the team-taught writers' workshop when one or the other was off campus, which was fairly frequently. Bill seized every opportunity to preach the gospel of poetry, and I commuted every other week to my family in Illinois, to readings and lectures of my own, and to duties as publisher–editor of Spoon River Poetry Press–Ellis Press, located in Peoria.

Spoon River Poetry Press–Ellis Press published not only *Spoon River Quarterly* but also chapbooks, small paperback books (several of which doubled as issues of the *Quarterly*), and hardback books. In 1984 I invented Plains Press, which I moved to Minnesota when my position at Southwest State became permanent. Plains Press absorbed both Spoon River Poetry Press and Ellis Press as imprints, but the two earlier presses had better name recognition, and only three books bear the Plains Press imprint: *Holiday: Minnesotans Remember the Farmers' Holiday Association*, by Dave Nass; *Bringing the Humanities to the Countryside*, by Gerrit Groen; and *The Music of Failure*, by Bill Holm.

Bill was the dominant figure on the Silver Dollar Bar–Cornstock scene and—when not on a grant-funded leave—a major presence at the university. His first book was as inevitable as Linda Hasselstrom's *Roadkill* and Leo Dangel's *Old Man Brunner Country*. A book by Bill Holm, I thought, would be a logical companion to the 1984 Farmers' Holiday book and an extension of my line of Spoon River Poetry Press–Ellis Press books celebrating the rural Midwest. Bill had a mountain of material beyond the boxelder bug poems, which Emilie Buchwald had taken for Milkweed Editions. I admired his strong language, his rural material, and his commitment to statement—none of this evasive, flip, avant-garde postmodern cuteness. Our agreement was simple and verbal: I would make the book, Bill could have all the free copies he wanted (my New York publishers had given me four author's copies, with more at the 40 percent "author's discount," which turns out to be the standard bookstore discount), and he would be in charge of its contents. If the disadvantage of small-press publication is low visibility, its advantage, I have always thought, is that authors control the contents of their own books. After a New York editor made the final chapter of *A Generation in Motion* say exactly the opposite of what I had written and really believe (on the grounds that reviewers "would not like" my critique of the seventies), I edit very little as an editor. Not that Bill did not seek and accept suggestions: one manuscript draft of "The Music of Failure," typed by our department secretary, has handwritten corrections/suggestions in at least four different inks. But in selecting contents for *The Music of Failure*, Bill Holm got whatever Bill Holm wanted. I did design the cover, based on a book I had bought in Czechoslovakia: one strong photograph superimposed on a map. I have used the design since on other books, and I like it: buried on those maps are a lot of subtle statements. The map in this case was a township-and-range map of Lyon County, Minnesota, showing the town of Minneota and, if you look closely, Bill's own house as well as the farmhouse I rented during my years in Minneota, south out of town across from St. Paul's Cemetery.

Usually I take my own photos, but in 1985 my file of southwest Minnesota photographs was still limited, so Bill's friend Tom Guttormsson provided photographs. And good ones they are. Tom also typeset the book at the office of the Minneota newspaper, the *Mascot*. Tom had already set several books for me, and I had flyers and advertising materials printed at the *Mascot*. At that time, typesetting had progressed beyond cold lead, but it had not yet reached the stage of electronic files. It was something a layman without a linotype machine could do, but it was tricky. A publisher prepared dummy pages called "camera-ready copy," which the printer converted to photographic negatives; those were burned onto an aluminum plate, which was then set on the drum of the offset press. The plates were recycled; film was stored against possible reprints. Camera-ready copy could be created in any way imaginable: on a typewriter, on a composing machine, even written out longhand, like some pages of (Ken) *Kesey's Garage Sale* (Viking, 1973). Justified prose (that is, lines with even left- and right-hand margins) was impossible on a typewriter and tricky on a composing machine (each line had to be typed twice), so the usual method for generating pasteups for a prose book was to have the text set photoelectrically and developed in long "galley" sheets, which were then cut to page size, waxed on the back, and pasted onto individual pages. (Those galleys faded if exposed to light or if the chemicals used in processing were not right.) Blue lines on the pasteup pages kept things more or less straight. Instructions to the printer were also written in blue, which does not photograph. Page numbers were pasted below the text and running heads pasted above. Symbols, design elements, and large letters for titles were available on "press type": sheets of transparent plastic full of letters or symbols, which could be positioned on the pasteup and then rubbed onto the page with a wooden stylus or knife handle. Alignment and spacing were always tricky, but I used press type for all book covers. Both galleys and pages could be proofread and corrected, with corrections being waxed, cut to a paragraph or a line or even a word, and pasted over the original. There was a real art to making pasteups, and if you look carefully at a book printed in this period, you can sometimes see a line of correction that was pasted in crooked.

I finished the pasteups for *The Music of Failure* the weekend of September 15, 1985, and gave page proofs to Bill for one last look.

With *Boxelder Bug Variations* already on its way, he was slightly distracted, so *The Music of Failure* was not approved for printing until October 5. I fretted some, because I wanted books by Christmas, but I found diversions with teaching, a major book fair in Chicago, and, early in November, with the death of Alec Bond, chair of the English department, a good poet and a good friend to both Bill and me. Still, by mid-November I had designed the flyer that announced *The Music of Failure* to the world; a bulk mailing of two thousand flyers, prepared over Thanksgiving vacation by my daughter Kristin, went out in early December, perhaps a month later than I would have liked. On the way back from Thanksgiving break in Peoria, I picked up *The Music of Failure* from M & D Printing in Henry, Illinois, and brought it to Minnesota. Having set Bill up with a phone call from Illinois about "a minor typographical problem on the cover, but nothing we can't live with," I took one copy of the book, soaked the cover enough for me to smudge the "u" and "s" out of the title, let the book dry, and, using the same press type I had used in making the cover pasteup, turned "The Music of Failure" into "The Magic of Failure." That was the copy I handed to an expectant Bill as soon as I saw him in Minneota, eliciting a barbaric yawp heard round the state. Even when I explained what I had done and showed him the real book, it took him about fifteen minutes to calm down.

All of us recognized Bill as a powerful figure in the local community, but we probably underestimated the larger audience he had built for himself during those many years of teaching, writing, and creating little stapled chapbooks like *Minnesota Lutheran Handbook* and *Happy Birthday Minneota*. By December 12, Bill had gone through seventy copies of *The Music of Failure* and needed more. In two short weeks the Marshall bookstore sold twenty, the Southwest State bookstore sold twenty, the *Mascot* sold eighteen, and Gustavus Adolphus

College (Bill's alma mater) had ordered twenty books. By January 8, 1986, my inventory was down to two hundred books. I ordered a quick reprint, adding blurbs by Robert Bly, Carol Bly, and Dave Etter to the back cover. The first printing was virtually gone by the time I sent out review copies in mid-January; I had barely enough books to service the reading and party Southwest State president Robert Carothers hosted for Bill on January 23. Even the reprint did not last long. Over a string of spring readings, Bill went through several boxes himself; Bookslinger, a major Midwest distributor, took one box after another; Elmer Suderman reviewed it in the *St. Paul Pioneer Press*; and *The Music of Failure* was named a Pushcart Press "Writer's Choice" selection. By May *The Music of Failure* was headed for its third printing of one thousand books. In the late 1980s, as I replaced Alec Bond as department chair and Bill headed off to China, the book held its own, as it did even into the late 1990s, when Plains Press had become but a footnote in publishing history.

During this time, *The Music of Failure*, or components thereof, reappeared several times. I included the title essay in the anthology *Late Harvest*, published by Paragon House in New York. (I was not embarrassed to include in that collection writers I myself had published, including Norbert Blei, Dave Etter, Linda Hasselstrom, Bill Kloefkorn, Leo Dangel, and Bill Holm ... and *Late Harvest* must have struck a nerve: it went into a paperback edition, and two printings of that, later to be pirated in an edition by one Marlowe & Company.) "The Music of Failure" reappeared again in Milkweed Editions' *The Heart Can Be Filled Anywhere on Earth*, which took its title from the essay's last line. The entire book was reprinted in 1987 under the title *Prairie Days* by Saybrook Publisher of New York, San Francisco, and Dallas. "Here's the old *Music of Failure* in fancy underwear," Bill wrote in my copy of that edition. The Saybrook printing is another funny story: at a book fair in New York City, I had picked up a subsidiary rights agent, Charlotte Gordon, who handled the *Late Harvest* negotiations and looked at all Spoon River Poetry Press–Ellis Press titles. Charlotte struck a deal with Saybrook for *The Music of Failure* contingent on a blurb from Garrison Keillor. Garrison generously delivered a blurb of exactly ninety-three words, including the oft-quoted remark about Bill's being "the tallest radical humorist in the Midwest" and a reference to Lake Wobegon. Saybrook then transformed the blurb into an "introduction," changed Bill's title from *The Music of Failure* to *Prairie Days* (because reviewers would be put off by the word *failure*), and designed a cover mirroring the cover of Keillor's *Lake Wobegon Days*. The typeface on "Bill Holm" is barely a smidgen larger than the typeface on "Introduction by Garrison Keillor." The price jumped to $13.95.

And now *The Music of Failure* reappears from the University of Minnesota Press, a quarter of a century after its initial publication. A book that survives this long is part of literary history, and to have been a part of such history—well, that is what small-press publishing is all about. An author survives in words buried in some library or dispersed in the amplitudes of the Internet. A teacher survives in his students' collective memory. A small-press publisher is validated when his author or book moves on up the publishing ladder. I am pleased to see *The Music of Failure* achieve a visibility I could never give it. I feel then that all the hours of making pasteups, writing grant proposals, packing books, and assembling bulk mailings were worthwhile, because I have left my little smudge on American literature, given some permanence to a really great moment—and recovered, as Mr. Dylan says, a place "when we were born in time." *Ave, frater, atque vale.*

BILL HOLM (1943–2009) was a one-of-a-kind poet, essayist, and musician. He wrote several acclaimed books and won the Minnesota Book Award and the McKnight Distinguished Artist Award. He lived in Minneota, Minnesota, and spent summers in Iceland, and he taught English for many years at Southwest Minnesota State University.

Best known for his short-short stories about "the boys," JIM HEYNEN has published poems, novels, nonfiction, and short fiction. He lives in St. Paul, Minnesota.

DAVID PICHASKE is professor of English at Southwest Minnesota State University. As editor in chief of Spoon River Poetry Press, Ellis Press, and Plains Press, he published many volumes of rural literature, including the first edition of *The Music of Failure*.